Floral Favorites

A collection of all-time favorite flowers featuring Hot Ribbon Applique

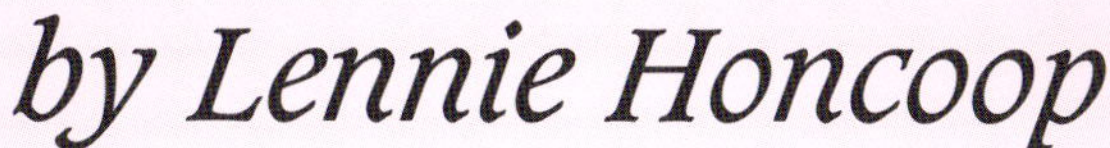

Acknowledgements

Author, quilt designer
Lennie Honcoop
Dutch Quilter
Elk Grove, California

Editor
Gary Honcoop
Dutch Quilter
Elk Grove, California

Photographer
Jeremy Cloud
Cloud Photography
Modesto, California

Technical Illustrator
Lisa Kirchoff
Hutchinson, Minnesota

Machine Quilter
Lennie Honcoop
Dutch Quilter
Elk Grove, California

Printer
Palmer Printing
St. Cloud, Minnesota

Publisher
Dutch Quilter
4105 Saul Court
Elk Grove, California

Table of Contents

Thank You

I am so blessed to have a group of people that continually go out of their way to support me with my quilt pattern designing work. Without them, my ideas for the patterns would still be just that – ideas. One always hesitates to publicly thank people because you run the risk of forgetting someone, but I owe most to the following.

First of all I want to thank my husband, Gary. He has the knack of taking the bits and pieces of ideas from my brainstorming and turning them into the sentences that express exactly what I was thinking but was not sure how to say. Of course after being married for 37 years, we should know each other pretty well! Although Gary claims to be "color-challenged," he is becoming a pretty good judge of which combination of colors look good in my patterns. He patiently listens to my uncertainties and doubts about the quality of my work and then tells me to "just do it!"

Next, I owe a huge debt of gratitude to John Darland and Ken O'Connell of Imagination International, Inc. for their encouragement and support over the past 6 years. They have been very generous in allowing me to use all the Hot Ribbon and Copic Markers I need. I would be remiss in not thanking the great crew working at Imagination International, Inc. who are always working hard to help me get all the supplies when I need them.

I do not think I would have been able to create my floral patterns if it were not for all the beautiful fabrics that Hoffman California Fabrics gave me. Sandy Muckenthaler has been especially helpful – always willing to show the new Hoffman fabrics and helping me pick those that I might be able to use. I am always excited when I get a delivery from Hoffman – I feel like a kid at Christmas as I look through the various fabrics I receive!

I have come to really appreciate Lora Kesilis of Baby Lock. She has been an enthusiastic supporter of my work. Her patience has been amazing as she taught me how to use the Baby Lock embroidery machine and serger that the Baby Lock Company gave me to use. Without her help, I would not be able to create the beautiful labels for my quilts.

Cheri Meineke-Johnson is another generous supporter. She has gladly supplied the Swarovski crystals that I like to use for adding a special touch to my patterns. The crystals are a great embellishment and help to make the pattern unique.

Finally, I am grateful beyond words to the doctor who restored my eyesight with lens transplants. Now I see clearly the flowers that I had only seen partially. I feel as if I have a new lease on life and I hope to use my new sight to continue discovering beautiful flowers that may inspire new patterns.

Lennie Honcoop

Introduction

MY INSPIRATION

I love flowers – that's obvious to anyone who knows me. After a day of planting flowers in my yard, I feel good because I know that I will soon be able to enjoy the beauty that each one will bring. I am in awe each time I see a particularly beautiful flower. But my love for flowers is more than just a feeling that comes as a reaction to a beautiful object. I have a strong sense that God is using flowers to smile at me! Flowers are some of the most beautiful pieces of God's creation and I want others to see and enjoy His flowers as I do.

I also love quilting fabrics; there is such a large variety of colors and types – batiks, florals, screen prints, and more. Being an artist by nature, I am so grateful that I can express my creativity and artistry by combining these two loves. My hope is that the beauty of flowers will inspire you to create many beautiful quilts.

MY CHALLENGE TO YOU

If this is your first exposure to my floral patterns, I would not be surprised if you told me that you find the patterns to be beautiful but too difficult for you to make. But if you can trace lines, cut out shapes, and color (the things you learned in kindergarten!), you CAN make any one of these patterns. You will be able to if you tell yourself you can.

I hope you will also learn to look at objects in a new way – not a casual glance or observation, but in a focused way. You will see colors, shapes, and shadows that were always there but you did not see. With that enhanced ability to see, you will have many new opportunities for creating beautiful quilts.

Dedication

To Gloria Ludgate, a very special person because she is a born cheerleader who encouraged and supported me when publishing Floral Fantasies. She has been an inspiration to me, especially now in her writings about her battle with cancer. When I think of who God may have sent as one of the angels to encourage us, Gloria has to be one of them!

Supplies

FABRICS

Use batiks, if at all possible, because they have the color variations that make it easier to fussy cut the exact color and shading for each piece of the pattern. The amount of fabric listed for a pattern allows for fussy cutting.

TOOLS

- Rotary cutter, ruler, and mat
- Sharpie marker (for tracing the pattern pieces)
- Two pair of scissors – a small sharp pair for precise trimming and a large pair
- A Clover Mini-Iron
- A large coffee mug (to park your mini-iron to avoid burns)
- Very fine steel wool (for cleaning the mini-iron)
- A regular iron (for heat setting)
- Straight pins and seam ripper
- Tweezers
- Sewing machine
- A padded surface, e.g., a June Taylor pressing board or folded towels

SUPPLIES

- Steam-a-Seam2 Light
- Bear Thread Appliqué Pressing Sheet
- Hot Ribbon
- Copic Markers
- Swarovski crystals
- Crystal heat setting tool
- Mary Ellen's Best Press (spray starch alternative)

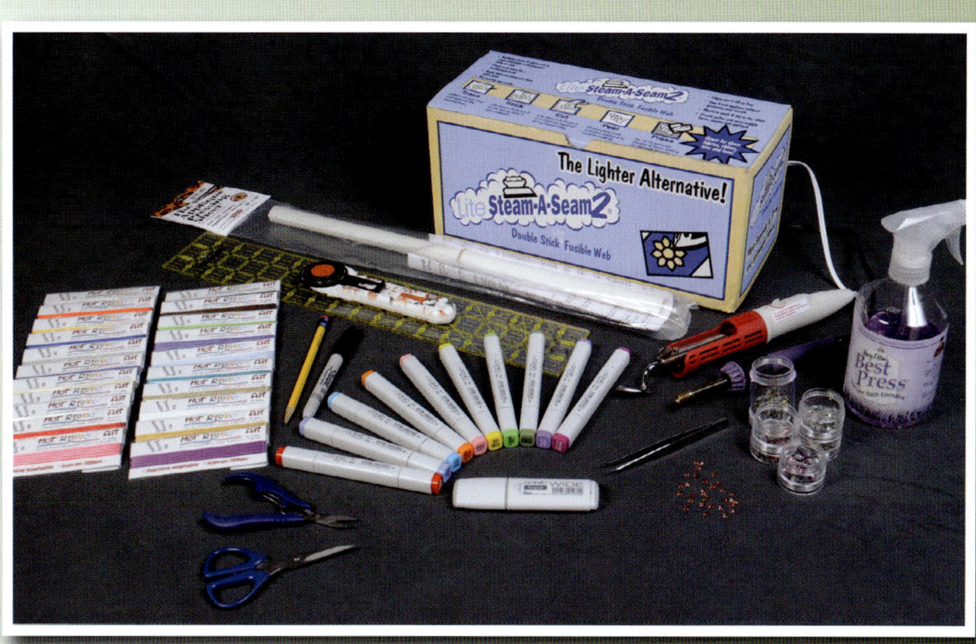

The Hot Ribbon Appliqué Technique

Traditional appliquéing has been around for a long time. I prefer using Hot Ribbon because it makes it so much easier and faster to finish the raw edges. In addition, Hot Ribbon gives me the results that I like – a sense of dimension and depth to my patterns. I can also alter the color of Hot Ribbon to get the shade of color that better matches (or complements) the fabric and give the effect that I am looking for.

TECHNIQUE STEPS

1. **Trace the pattern pieces on Steam-a-Seam2.** Place a sheet of Steam-a-Seam2 over the pattern and trace the pieces. Copy any numbers or other marks shown on the pattern piece.

2. **Cut the pieces out roughly, i.e., not precisely on the line.** Leave at least 1/8" of fusible material around each pattern piece.

3. **Remove the backing paper and press the pieces to the back of the fabric.** Look at the fabric carefully and find the right spots to use for the large and important pieces.
   Darker areas: Use them for parts of flower petals near the center of a flower, or for leaves that are in the shadows.
   Streaks: Decide which direction streaks would go on a real leaf or petal, and take advantage of any streaks in the fabric. You can finger press the pieces in place. If a piece does not adhere, you can use a warm iron to very lightly press the pieces to reactivate the adhesive.
   That's one reason I like Steam-a-Seam2.
   TIP: If the paper is difficult to remove, score it in the center with a sharp object, such as a straight pin.

4. **Cut out pieces carefully.** Carefully cut out each piece – I recommend cutting on the outside of the tracing line – it gives some room to work with when putting into place.

5. **Enlarge the placement guide by the percent noted with each placement guide.** Use a photocopier to enlarge the placement guide. If the pattern is too large to fit the largest sheet available for the copier, you can copy in sections and then overlap the sections so the parts match; tape together to hold in place.

6. **Place the Bear Thread Appliqué Pressing Sheet over the enlarged placement guide.** It's okay if the pressing sheet is a little smaller than the placement guide. It should, however, cover at least a part of each flower petal and leaf. Tape the pressing sheet to the placement guide in a couple of places to keep it from shifting. Avoid having the tape cover any of the design lines.

7. **Place each piece in the spot on the placement guide that has a number/letter that corresponds to the number/letter on the cut out piece.** Peel the paper backing off each piece and place it in the designated spot on the pressing sheet. Start with back pieces. If you gently finger press the pieces in place, you will be able to reposition them if you need to. Some pieces will overlap each other and some might go beyond the edge of the pressing sheet. There may be some distortion in the placement guide from being enlarged, which might cause some pieces to be farther apart or closer together than shown in the drawing. That is not a problem because the placement guide is just that – a guide. You can make your arrangement any way you want it. After all pieces have been placed, iron them to the pressing sheet.
NOTE: Let the pieces cool before attempting to remove your pattern – if the pieces are not cool, you may distort the fabric.

8. **Transfer the design to the background fabric.** Remove the design from the appliqué sheet and place on the background fabric. Press with hot iron to set it in place. NOTE: *When placing your design on the background fabric, leave more open space at the top than the bottom.*

Applying Hot Ribbon

Hot Ribbon is a 1/8" wide laser-cut strip of polyester with heat-activated adhesive on the back. Hot Ribbon, which comes in 22 colors, is great for finishing the edges of appliqué and creating depth and dimension to your pattern that makes it distinctive and impressive. Just tack it in place with a mini-iron and heat set with a hot iron to make it permanently adhere.

1. **Choose the best color of Hot Ribbon.** Listed with each project are the colors of Hot Ribbon that I used; if your fabric is a different color, choose the color that best matches your fabric. If I can not find a good match of Hot Ribbon to my fabric, I often use the color White for creating softer pastels and Gray for muted colors. I can shade any Hot Ribbon with a permanent marker (I use Copic Markers) to subtly blend colors. You can color the Hot Ribbon before or after applying it to the fabric.

2. **Preheat the Clover Mini-Iron on a medium setting (about "2 o'clock" on the mini-iron dial).** The metal part of the mini-iron is very hot; when you are are not using it, make sure you place it where you won't burn yourself. I like to use a large coffee mug.

3. **Apply the Hot Ribbon.** Making sure the adhesive (dull) side is down, place the Hot Ribbon at a starting point, covering the edge of the appliqué. Leave the mini-iron on the Hot Ribbon for just a few seconds to tack in place.

- Guide the Hot Ribbon gently (don't pull it!) where you want it placed, while sliding the mini-iron slowly over the Hot Ribbon.

- To go around gentle curves, bend the Hot Ribbon in the direction you want to go, taking very tiny "steps." Because the heat from the mini-iron will soften the adhesive in Hot Ribbon, the Hot Ribbon will bend easily. You need to find the right amount of pressure in moving the Hot Ribbon around curves – moving it without pulling it.

- Avoid "layering" Hot Ribbon. If you make a mistake or change your mind on the color or placement of the Hot Ribbon, reheat the Hot Ribbon, pull it gently off, and replace it with a new piece.

4. **Bond permanently**. The mini-iron only "tacks" the Hot Ribbon in place. YOU MUST HEAT SET IT to bond it permanently. Using a pressing sheet, iron each spot on your pattern with a hot iron for 10-12 seconds; repeat 3 to 4 times for a total of 35-40 seconds on each spot. Once heat set, your project is washable (handle it as you would any delicate fabric). DO NOT PUT in a hot dryer. If your project is accidently exposed to heat and the Hot Ribbon comes loose, use a hot iron with a pressing sheet to "re-set" it.

TIPS:

Making sharp corners with Hot Ribbom

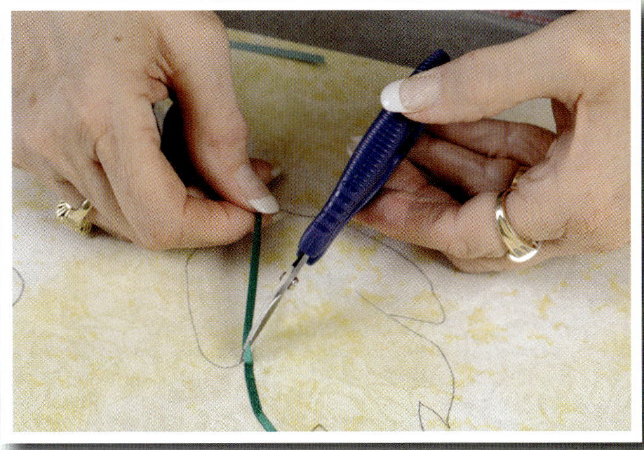

1, Snip the end at an angle as shown.

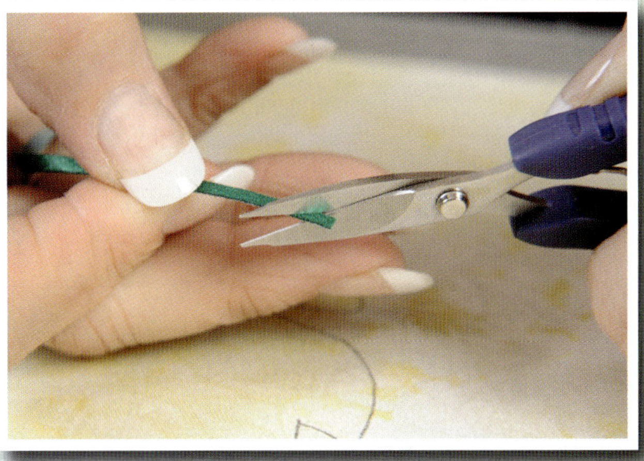

2, Cut the end at an opposite angle.

3. Place next to (not over) the first piece.

Transitioning from one color to another

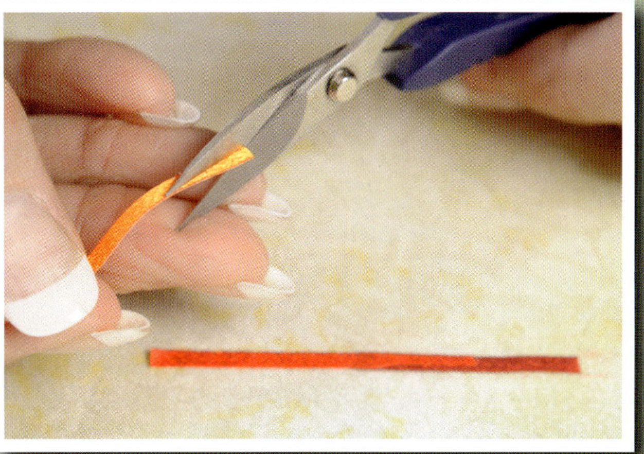

1. Make a long tapered cut.

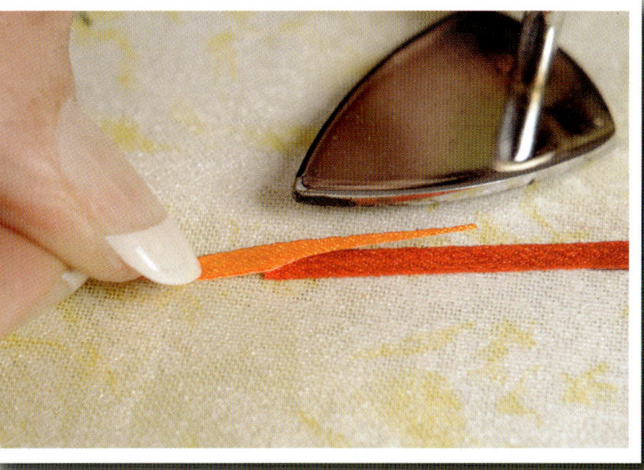

2. Place over the other piece as shown.

Enhancing your Project with Copic Markers

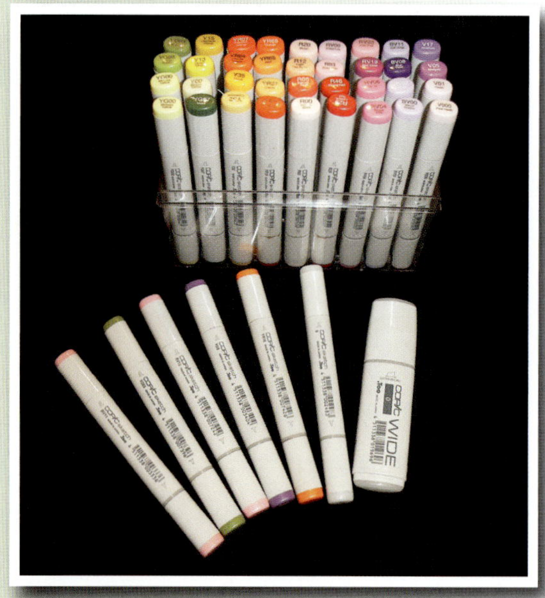

Copic markers are a commercial grade illustrator pen that works wonderfully for coloring Hot Ribbon and fabric. The pens contain a permanent dye in an alcohol compound that dries quickly and acid free and comes in over 320 colors. Because the colors are transparent, you can use them as you would water colors in that you can blend them to create the exact color, shade, or hue that you want. Another benefit of being transparent is that the underlying fabric is not covered/hidden when you use Copic Markers on it.

NOTE: *Copic markers can be used to alter or darken the color of a fabric – they can not change the fabric to a lighter color.*

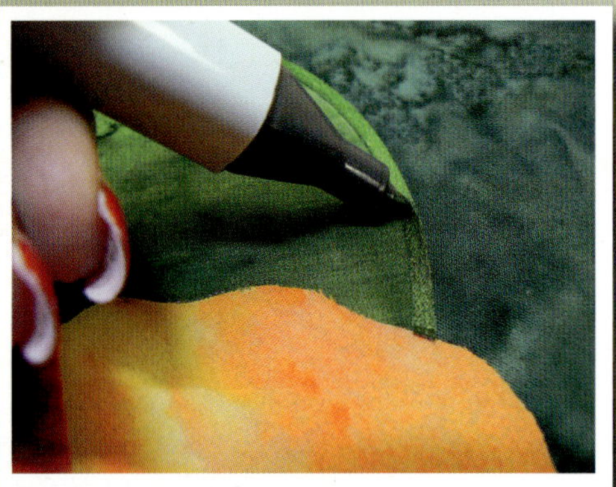

I use Copic markers for several purposes:

1. **Altering the color of Hot Ribbon.** Hot Ribbon is available in 22 colors; fabric, however, comes in an almost infinite number of colors and patterns. I use a Copic Marker to alter the color of the Hot Ribbon to better match the color of the adjoining fabric.

2. **Adding highlights to the fabric.** Copic Markers work well on fabrics also and allow me to add highlights to certain parts of a flower to give the sense of depth or to a leaf to depict a shadow.

3. **Depicting a color transition.** One of the Copic Markers available is a Colorless Blender, which contains the alcohol compound but no dye. I can use the blender pen to soften a color. I can also show a transition of one color to another – I put a color on the fabric and as I "draw it out," I add small amounts of another color and work it in. The Angel Trumpets pattern in my earlier book, *Floral Fantasies*, is an excellent example of how I was able to transition one color into another.

With each pattern, I have listed the Copic Markers I used with that pattern. Although I note that Copic Markers are optional, I would encourage you to try them because you will able to add enhancements that will make your quilt special.

Embellishing with Swarovski Crystals

One embellishment that I have come to love is Swarovski crystals. I use them to depict the reflection of sunlight on a petal or the presence of drops of dew on a leaf or flower. In other cases, I add the crystals because I want the flower to sparkle, to call attention to itself. There are various types of crystals available but I prefer Swarovski because I find them to be of higher quality.

Adding Swarovski crystals to your project is pretty straightforward.

1. Select a color that accomplishes the effect you want. The crystals are wonderful for enhancing the center of a flower, especially the darker colors. Crystals help to convey vividly the stamen in the center of a flower. Some parts of flower may look less appealing than another; but by adding some clear crystals, you bring it to life.

2. Use the proper tools. You will need a special heat setting tool (I recommend the one available from Cheri's Crystals) and a pair of tweezers.

3. Place the crystal in its desired location and apply heat. Pick up a crystal with a pair of tweezers; place it in the spot you selected; and apply the heat setting tool for 10 seconds for small crystals and 12 seconds for large crystals. After the crystal has cooled, it is permanent.

Finishing Your Quilt

The gorgeous little one is my youngest granddaughter, Emily, who looks like she's thinking about being a top quilter.

Choosing Border Fabrics

The best way to chose borders for your project is take your quilt to a fabric shop or lay it out in the room where you keep your stash of materials and try out different possible combinations of fabrics. Many times using the background fabric as the outer border helps to "tie" the project together. However, make sure that the borders do not distract from the pattern – you want the focus to be on the pattern. The borders should provide a subtle enhancement, just like a frame does for a photograph.

Adding Borders

1. **Choose the fabrics** (see above).
2. **Square up the design.** Measure through the middle and at each end. Trim as needed.
3. **Add inner borders:**

   Side Borders
   - Cut two strips the length of your quilt and the width of your choice
   - Sew them to the side of the design
   - Press the seams

   End Borders
   - Measure the width, including the side borders
   - Cut two strips that length and the width of your choice
   - Sew them to the top and bottom of the design
   - Press
4. **Add outer borders:**

   Side Borders
   - Measure the length, including the inner borders
   - Cut two strips that length and the width of your choice
   - Sew them in place
   - Press

   End Borders
   - Measure the width, including the borders
   - Cut two strips that length and the selected width
   - Sew them to the top and bottom of the design
   - Press

Top Quilting

Because of multiple layers of fabric and fusible web in some places, hand quilting would be very difficult. I strongly recommend that the project be machine quilted. If you plan to do the top quilting yourself, here are tips and suggestions.

Get Everything Ready

- Press the quilt top; square up on all four sides; and remove all loose threads.
- Cut the batting at least 1" larger than the quilt top on each side. If you are using a long-arm machine or quilting frame, the batting should extend 2" to 4" on each side.
- Cut the backing the same size as or slight larger than the batting.
- If you will be quilting with a small sewing machine, baste or pin layers together with medium size safety pins every few inches. If you have a long-arm machine, stretch the design on the quilting frame.

Quilt with a Free-Motion Technique

- Start at the center and outline any small shapes where there is no design; stitch right next to the Hot Ribbon outline, but do NOT stitch over Hot Ribbon.
- Outline the whole cluster, again stitching near the Hot Ribbon.
- Quilt a design of your choice in the inner border
- Fill up the background with stippling –continuous curving lines meandering randomly
- Quilt the outer border in a design of your choice
- Do a small amount of quilting in the design area to help the project to lie flat; try to stitch lines that enhance the design

Adding a Sleeve

Since this is wall hanging, you will want to have a nice hanging sleeve.

1. Cut a wide strip. From the same fabric as the backing, cut a 9" wide strip the length of the top edge of the quilt. (Quilt shows usually require 4" finished sleeves.)
2. Stitch up the ends. Fold the strip with the right sides together. Stitch up the ends about 1½" from the edge of the quilt. Turn right side out and press.
3. Sew to the back of the quilt with a ¼" seam.
4. Slip-stitch the folded edge to the quilt. The raw edge will be covered by the binding.

Binding the Edges

There are many ways to do binding, so use your favorite technique. Here's mine.

1. Spread out the quilt and trim carefully. Square up the quilt exactly. There are folding rulers available that are great for squaring up your quilt.
2. Make strips for binding. Cut strips 2½' wide, the length of each side plus 2" on each end. I use straight strips because bias strips do not hold their shape. Fold each strip over, wrong sides together, and iron.
3. Stitch them in place. Sew a doubled strip to each side, on the front of the quilt, with the raw edge ¼" in from the edge of the quilt top. Start and stop ¼" from the corner.
4. Miter the corners. Miter the corners by machine. (Practice this on pot-holder size projects first.)
5. Fold the binding to the back and stitch neatly by hand with a blind stitch.

Adding a Label

There are a number of ways to make a label. One is to simply write with an indelible pen on a piece of fabric the information you want to include: who made it, when it was made, what special significance it may have.

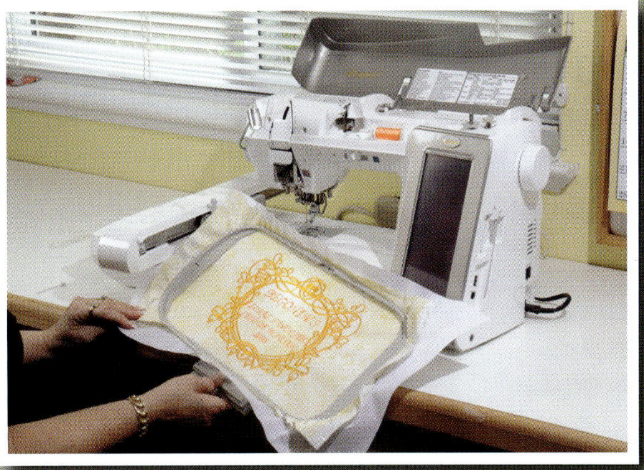

I embroider my labels with my Baby Lock Ellegante2 because I then have a wide range of embellishments available to make the label match/complement the quilt.

California Poppies

California Poppies have a special place in my heart.
I will always remember when I saw my first California Poppies. The first spring after immigrating to California from The Netherlands we were sightseeing in the Sierra foothills when I saw roadsides and fields with California Poppies in full bloom. What a glorious sight! Their bright colors symbolized perfectly for me the new beginning that I had in California.

California Poppies

34" x 34"

Fabric & Supplies

Refer to page 7 for recommendations on Fabrics, Tools, and Supplies.

Fabric Requirements

¾ yd - Outer Border and Binding
2/3 - Background (mottled royal blue)
¼ yd - Inner border (mottled orange)
¼ yd - Inner border (green)
¼ yd - Leaves (light gray-green)
1/3 yd - Flowers (mottled orange)
1-1/8 yds - Backing (color of your choice)

Hot Ribbon

3 pkgs - #11 Lime Green
2 pkgs - #13 Orange
3 pkgs - #19 Golden Yellow

Copic Ciao Markers *(Optional)*

1 - YG63 Pea Green
1 - YR07 Cadmium Orange
1 - 0 Colorless Blender

Swarovksi Crystals *(Optional)*

50 - #13 Ernite
25 - #17 Hyacinth
30 - #18 Jet Black
30 - #37 Sun

Cutting Instructions

1. **Background:**
   Cut one 24" x 24" square
2. **Orange Inner Border:**
   Cut four 2" strips
3. **Green Inner Border:**
   Cut four 1¼" strips
4. **Royal Blue Outer Border:**
   Cut four 4" strips
5. **Binding:**
   Cut four 2½" strips

Constructing the Quilt

Refer to **The Hot Ribbon Applique Technique** on page 8 for step by step instructions.

Embellish your quilt with Swarovski Crystals. Detailed instructions on page 13.

California Poppies Placement Guide

This diagram has been reduced.
Use for template placement only.

Enlarge Placement Guide 220%

Templates have been reversed for tracing purposes.

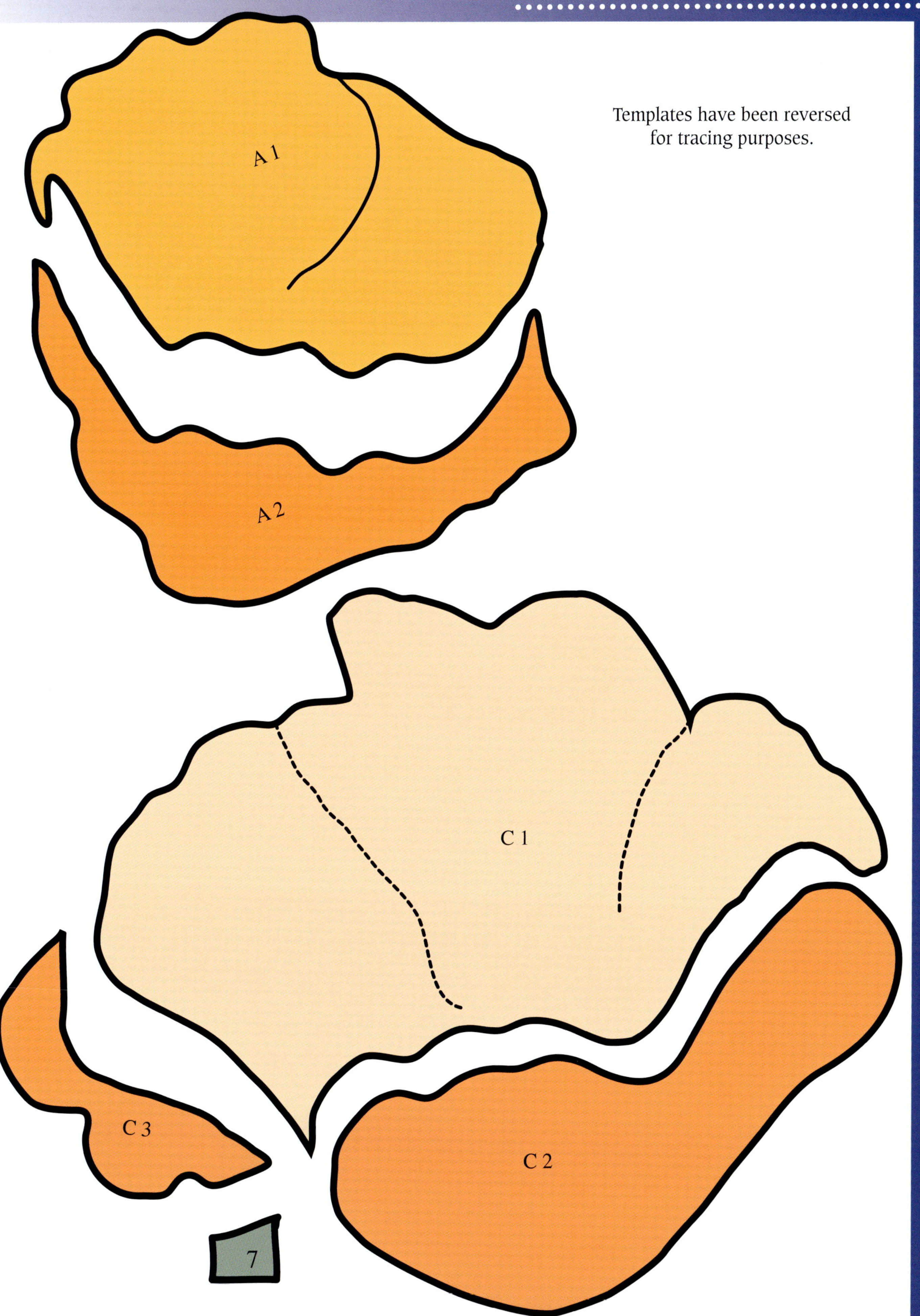

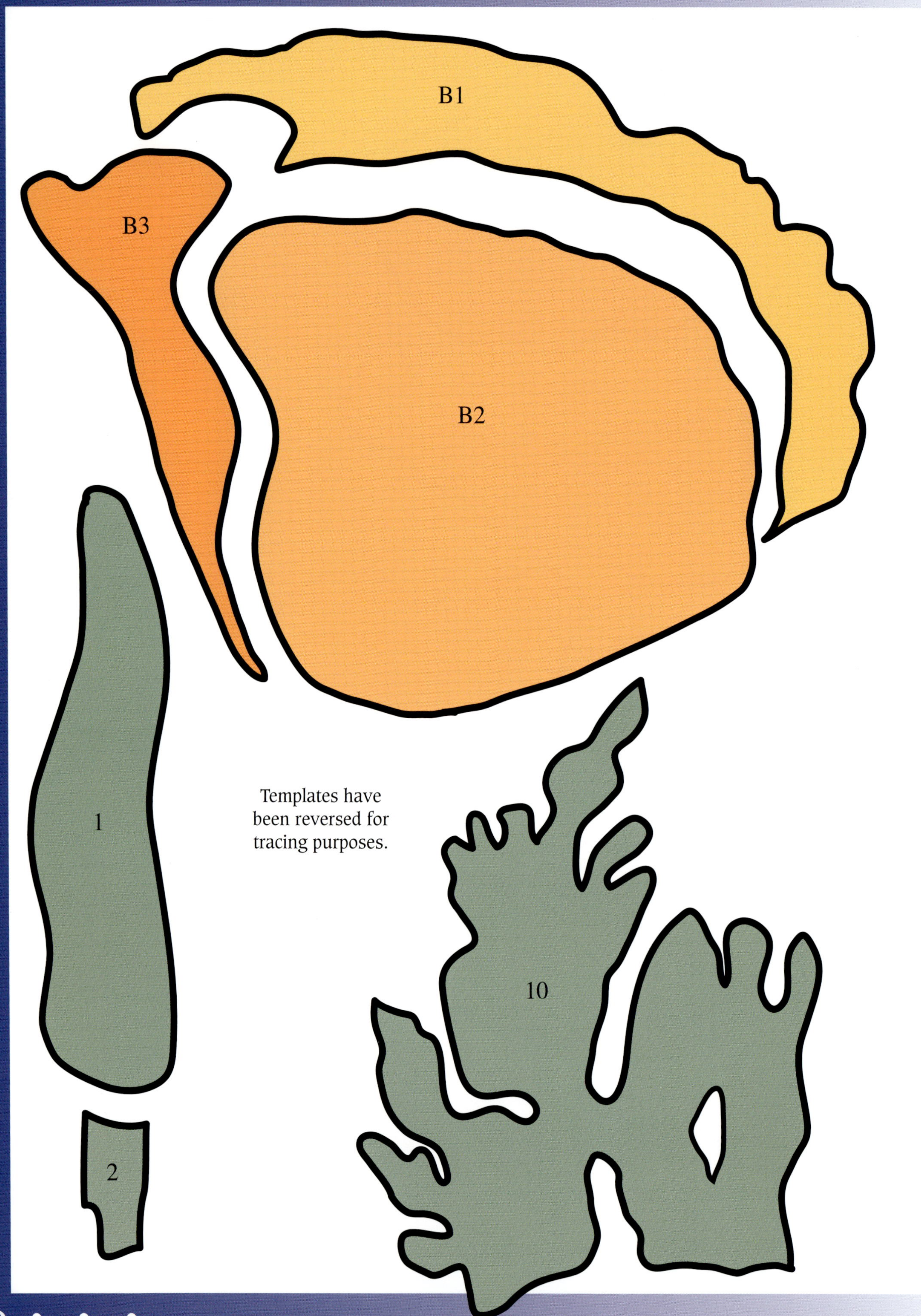

Templates have
been reversed for
tracing purposes.

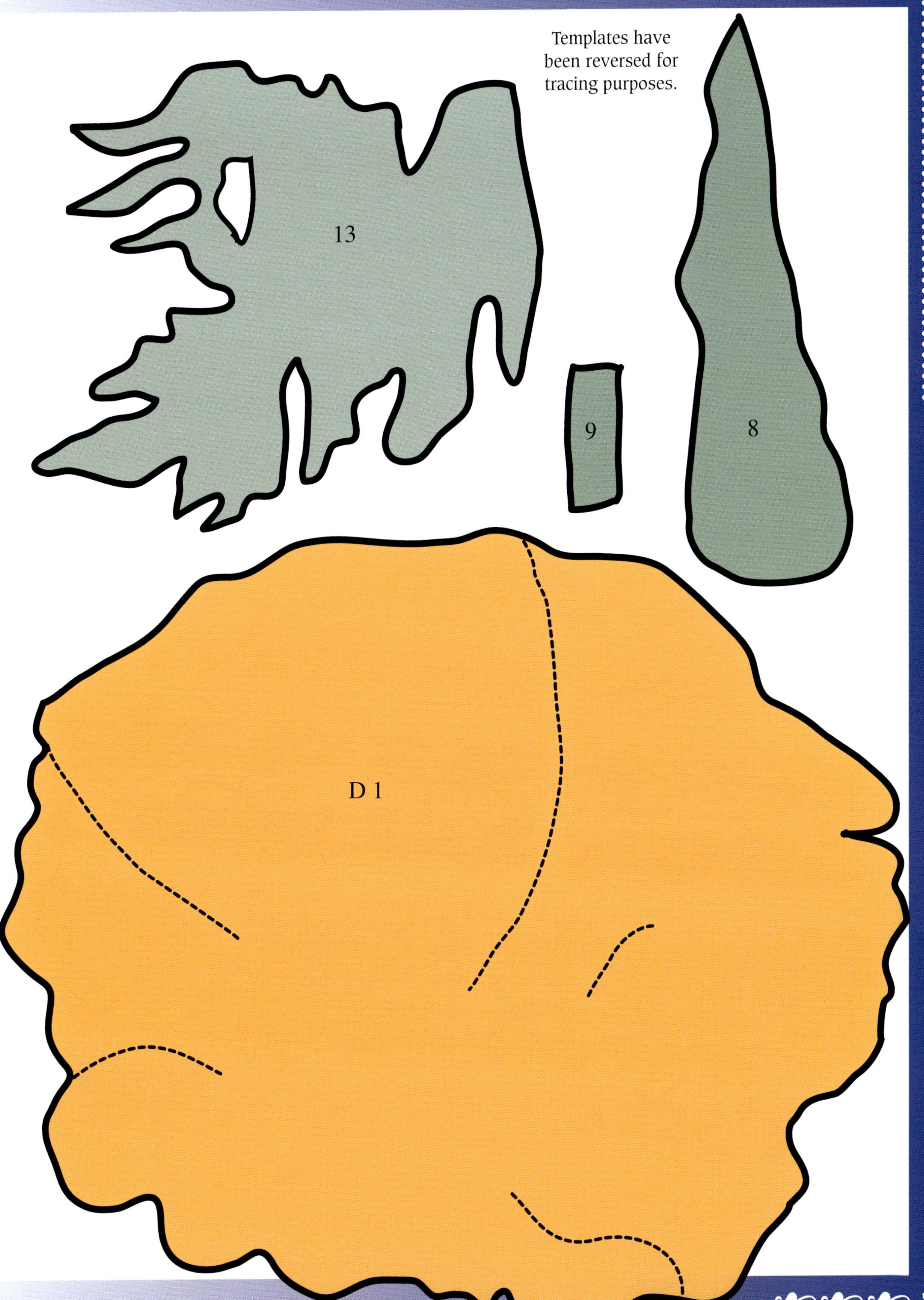
Templates have
been reversed for
tracing purposes.
13
9
8
D 1

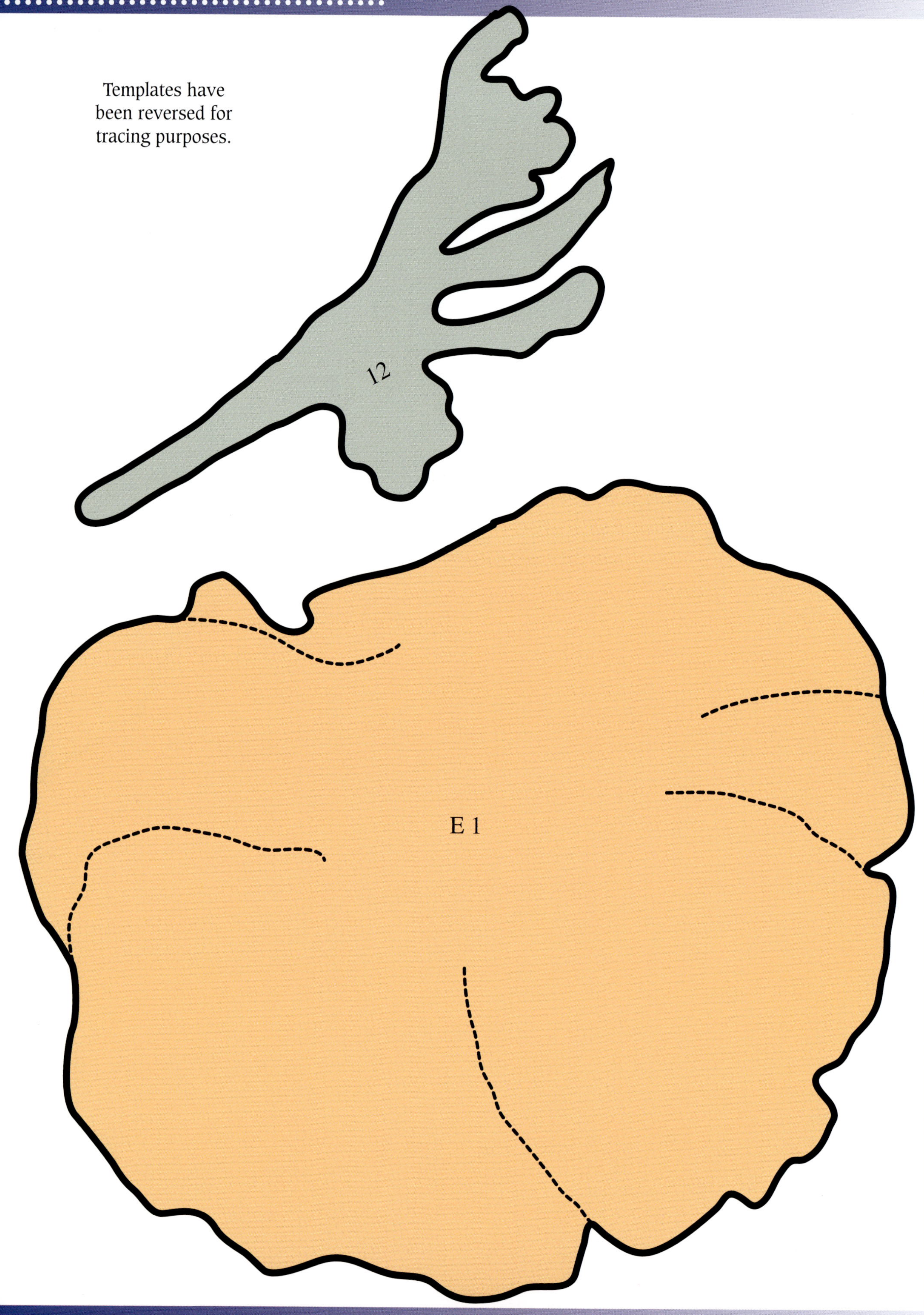
Templates have
been reversed for
tracing purposes.
12
E 1

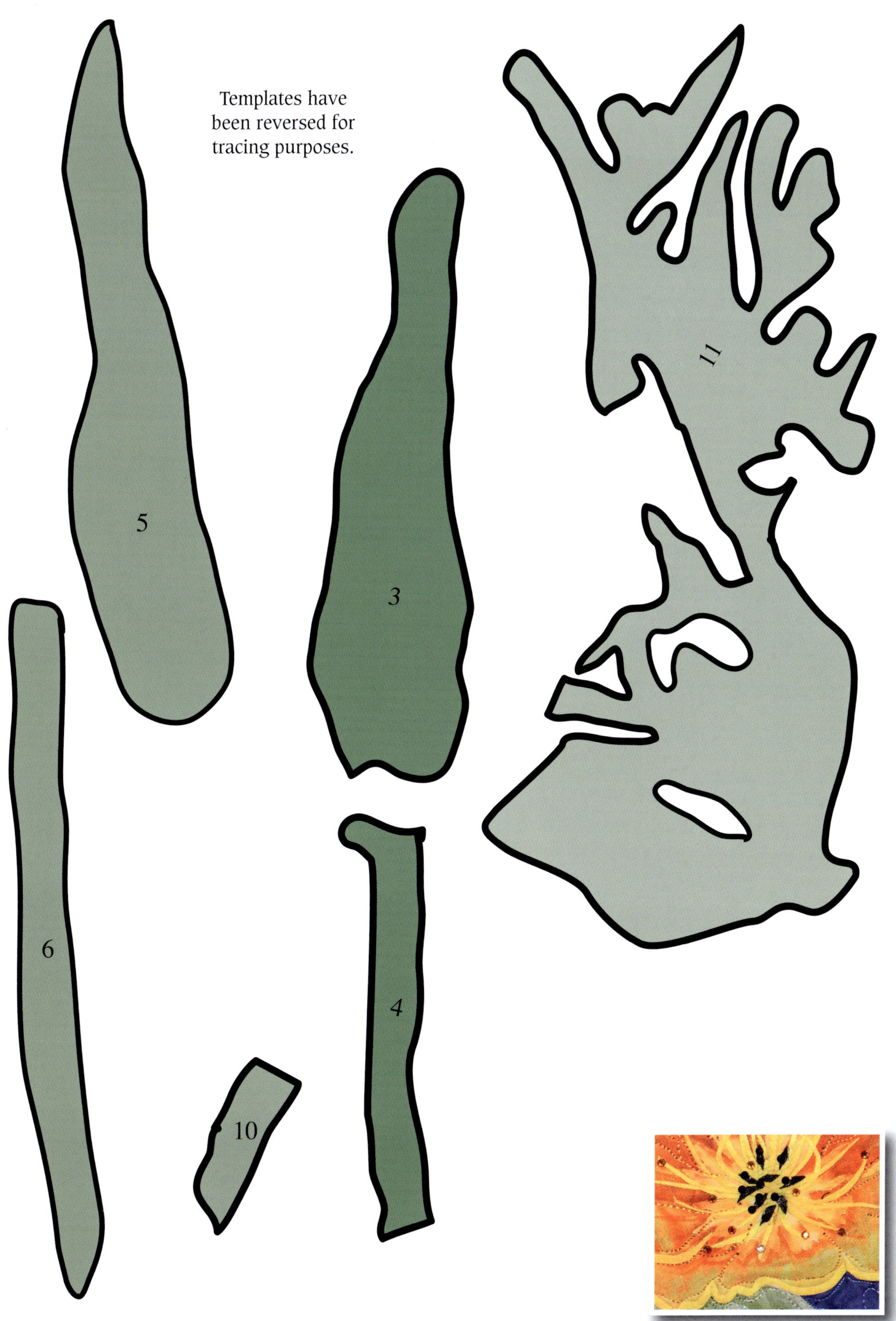
Templates have
been reversed for
tracing purposes.
5
3
11
6
4
10

Begonias

*Begonias are another one of my favorite flowers.
They have intense colors yet seem to have a translucence about them that adds to their appeal.
I have some recall of seeing begonias in The Netherlands but never paid much attention to them
until I was "formally" introduced to them by a friend who brought me several plants from a nursery near Santa Cruz.
I was "hooked" on begonias after I saw the flowers and discovered that they bloom through the summer.
Several years ago I had the opportunity to stop at the same begonia nursery near Santa Cruz and found
it was having a closing sale. I was strongly advised by the nursery staff not to waste my money buying any
plants because "begonias do not grow in hot climates." I'm happy that I did not take their advice
because I now have a number of hanging baskets with begonias that I'm able to enjoy.*

Begonias

42" x 42"

Fabric & Supplies

Refer to page 7 for recommendations on Fabrics, Tools, and Supplies.

Fabric Requirements

1 yd – Background (black)

1 yd – Outer Border and binding (black)

1/3 yd – Inner Border (green leaf print)

1/8 yd – Inner Border (peach)

¼ yd – Flowers (mottled pink)

¼ yd – Flowers (mottled apricot)

¼ yd – Flowers (mottled yellow)

1/3 yd – Leaves (mottled green)

1½ yds – Backing (color of your choice)

Hot Ribbon

6 pkgs – #1 White - if coloring your own Hot Ribbon for the flowers.
If not, then:

- 2 pkgs – #2 Red
- 2 pkgs – #8 Lemon Yellow, and
- 2 pkgs – #13 Orange

3 pkgs – #14 Forest Green

1 pkg – #20 Dark Brown

Copic Ciao Markers *(Optional)*

1 – YG67 Moss Green

1 – YR02 Light Orange

1 – YR61 Yellowish Skin Pink

1 – Y11 Pale Yellow

1 – R05 Salmon Red

1 – 0 Colorless Blender

Swarovksi Crystals *(Optional)*

24 – #17 Hyacinth

50 – #37 Sun

24 – #11 Crystal

8 – #7 Citrine

24 – #9 Coral Pink

6 – #39 Lt. Topaz (large)

6 – #7 Citrine (large)

Cutting Instructions

1. **Background:**
   Cut one 30½" x 30½" rectangle
2. **Green Inner Border:**
   Cut four 2½" strips
3. **Peach Inner Border:**
   Cut four 1" strips
4. **Black outer border:**
   Cut five 4" strips
5. **Binding:**
   Cut five 2½" strips

Constructing the Quilt

Refer to **The Hot Ribbon Applique Technique** on page 8 for step by step instructions.

Begonias Placement Guide

This diagram has been reduced.
Use for template placement only.

Enlarge Placement Guide 250%

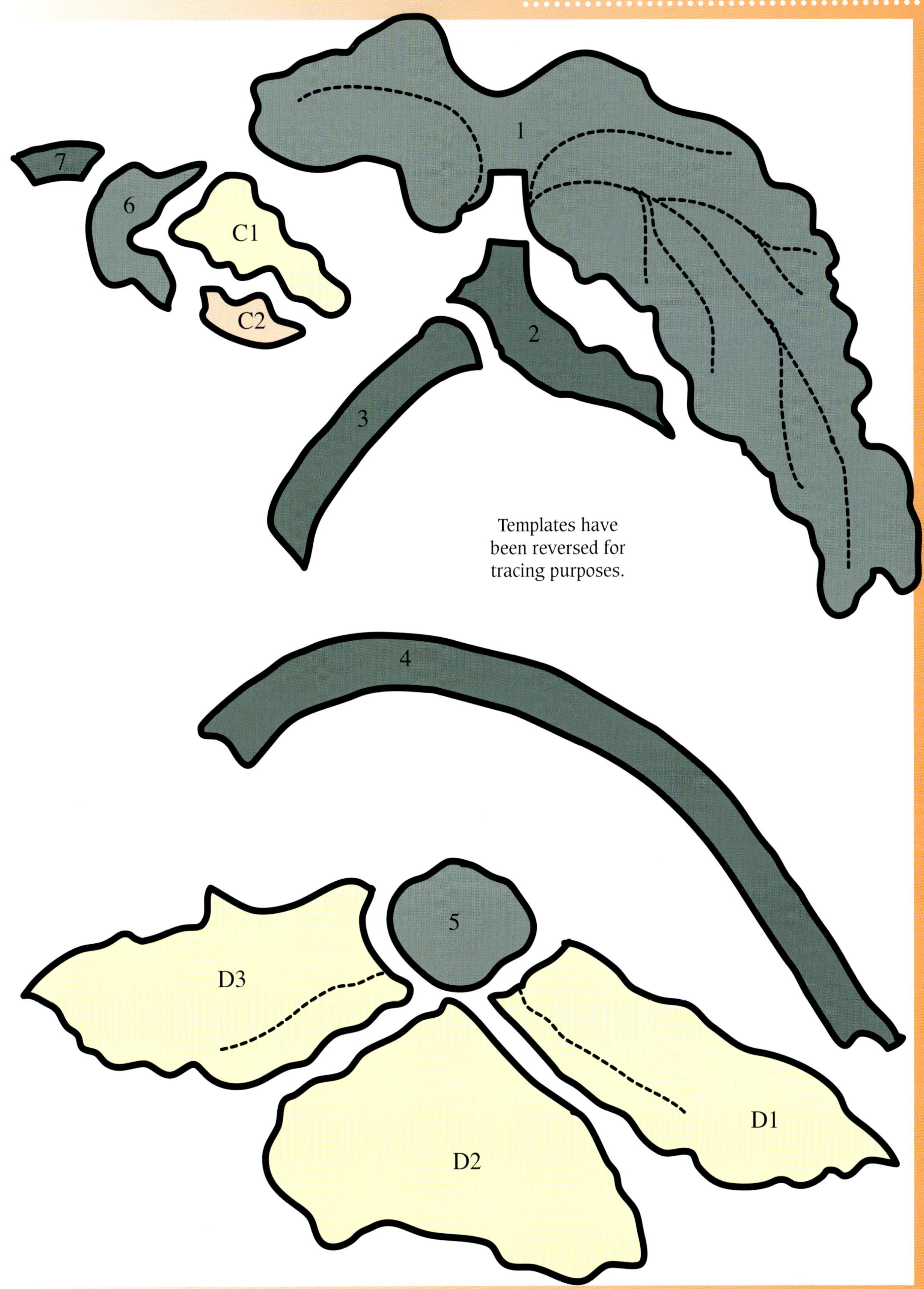
1
7
6
C1
C2
2
3
Templates have
been reversed for
tracing purposes.
4
5
D3
D2
D1

Templates have been reversed for tracing purposes.

Templates have been reversed for tracing purposes.

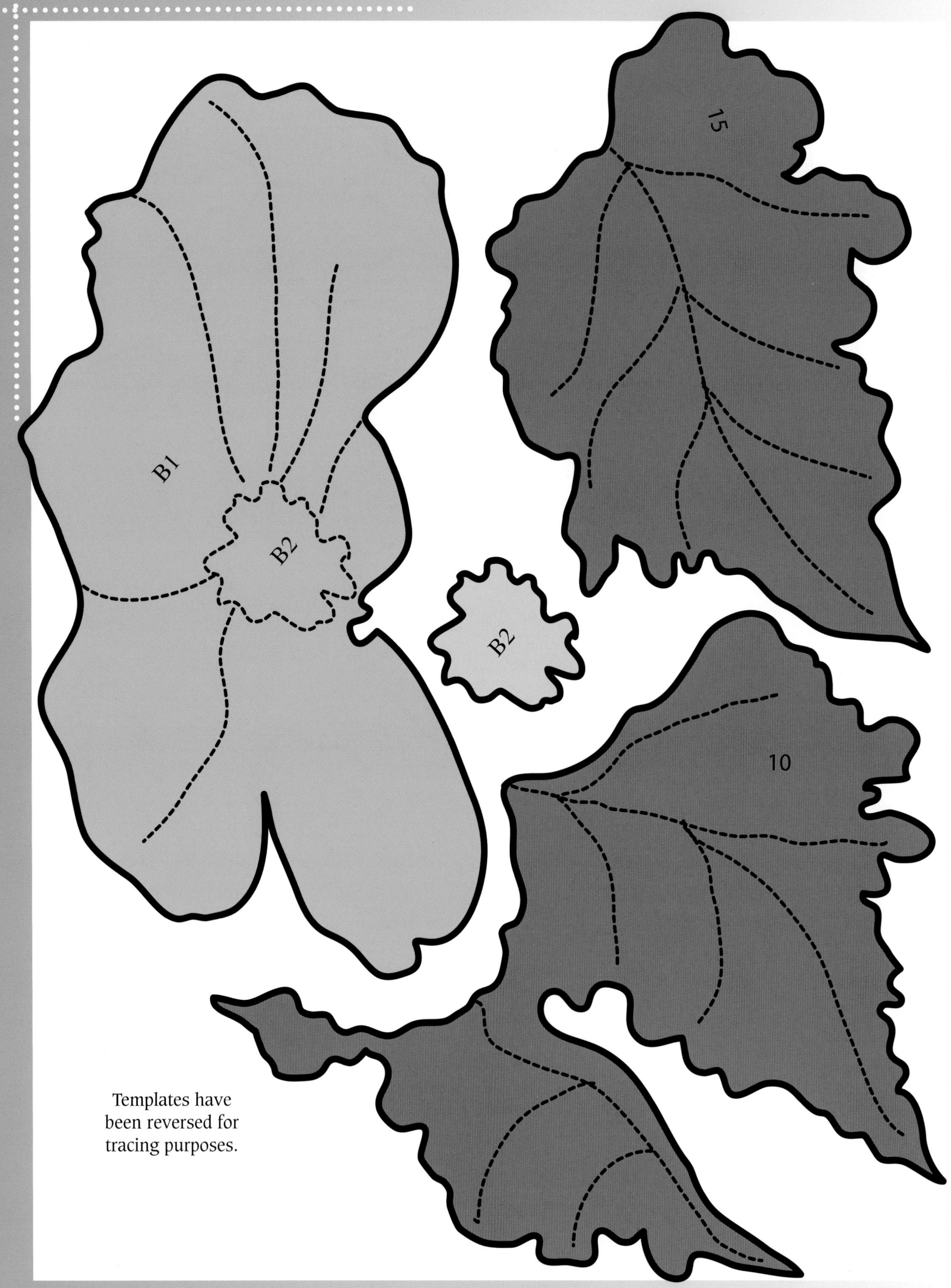
15
B1
B2
B2
10
Templates have been reversed for tracing purposes.

Templates have been reversed for tracing purposes.

Christmas Cactus

A Christmas cactus brings back memories of Christmas as a child in The Netherlands. Christmas cactus plants were used to decorate tables during the holiday season. I have a long history with this flower as I still have Christmas cactus plants on the window sill in my studio. One of the plants grew from a piece of a Christmas cactus plant that my mother-in-law gave me when I had just immigrated to California – that's more than 37 years ago!! It always amazes me that the more I neglect a cactus plant, the more beautiful flowers it seems to produce! What a lesson to learn – we do not have to be the center of attention before we can "blossom." God expects us to blossom in all circumstances so we can bring joy and beauty to those around us.

Christmas Cactus

36" x 36"

Fabric & Supplies

Refer to page 7 for recommendations on Fabrics, Tools, and Supplies.

Fabric Requirements

¾ yd – background (black with gold polka dots)
¾ yd – outer border and binding (Christmas print)
¼ yd – inner border (salmon)
¼ yd – inner border (red)
1/3 yd – flowers (mottled light peach)
¼ yd – leaves (green)
1¼ yds – backing (color of your choice)

Hot Ribbon

4 pkgs – #1 White
3 pkgs – #11 Lime Green
1 pkg – #17 Hot Pink

Copic Ciao Markers *(Optional)*

1 – YG63 Pea Green
1 – YR61 Yellowish Skin Pink
1 – YR02 Flesh
1 – RV02 Sugar Almond Pink
1 – 0 Colorless Blender

Swarovksi Crystals *(Optional)*

60 – #22 Light Peach
10 – #22 Light Peach (large)
10 – #9 Coral Pink
15 – #17 Hyacinth
48 – #29 Peridot

Cutting Instructions

1. **Background:**
   Cut one 24" x 24" square
2. **Red Inner Border:**
   Cut four 2" strips
3. **Peach Inner Border:**
   Cut four 1¼" strips
4. **Christmas Print Outer Border:**
   Cut four 4½" strips
5. **Christmas Print Binding:**
   Cut four 2½" strips

Constructing the Quilt

Refer to **The Hot Ribbon Applique Technique** on page 8 for step by step instructions.

Christmas Cactus Placement Guide

This diagram has been reduced.
Use for template placement only.

Enlarge Placement Guide 250%

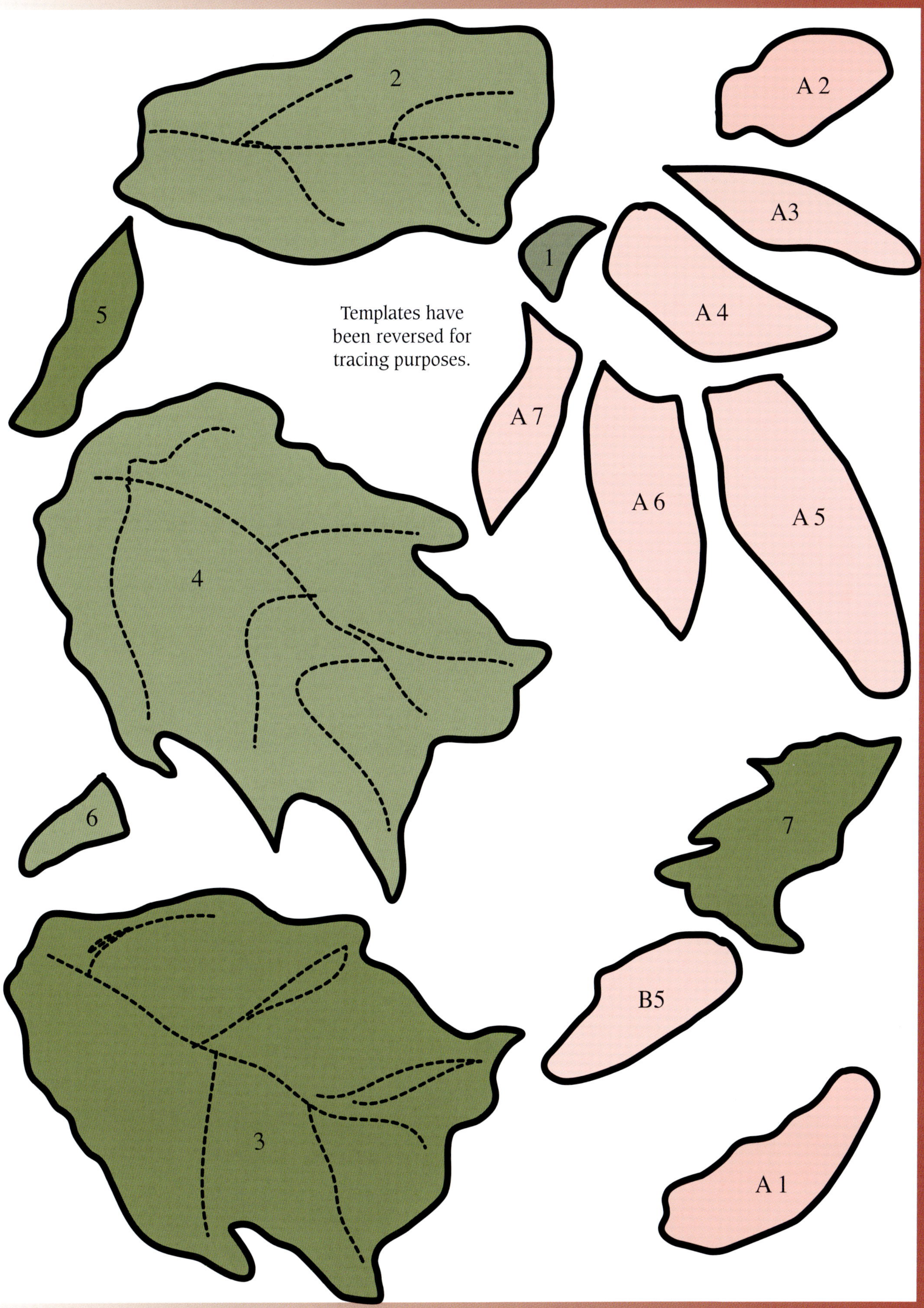

Templates have been reversed for tracing purposes.

Templates have been reversed for tracing purposes.
B1
12
B2
8
10
B3
13
11
B4
9
14

Templates have been reversed for tracing purposes.

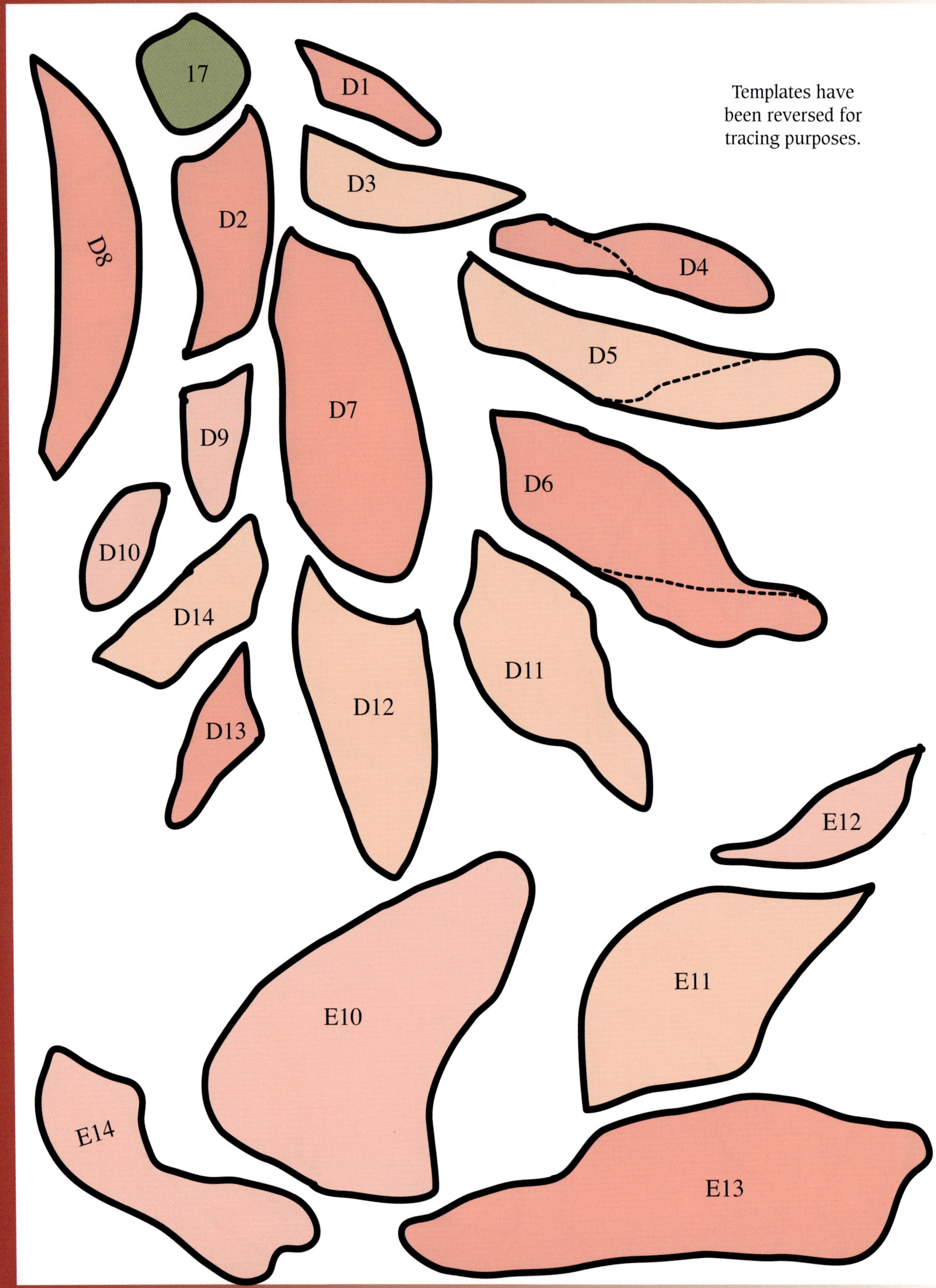
17
D1
Templates have been reversed for tracing purposes.
D3
D8
D2
D4
D5
D7
D9
D6
D10
D14
D11
D12
D13
E12
E10
E11
E14
E13

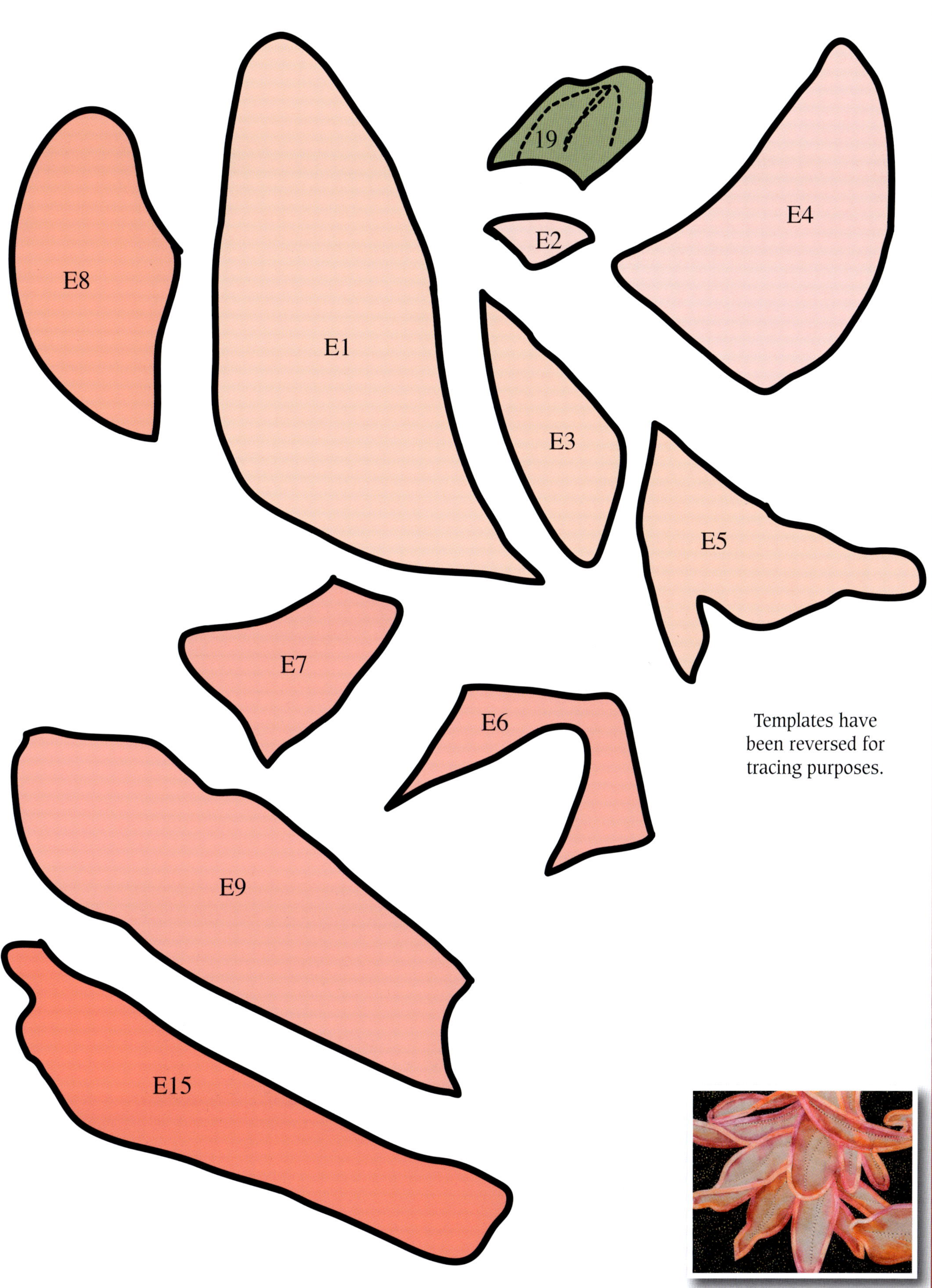

Templates have been reversed for tracing purposes.

Gladiolas

Gladiolas are a special flower to me in a very personal way. Gladiolas were the favorite flower of my father-in-law whom I loved dearly. With his Dutch heritage, it is not surprising that gladiolas were my father-in-law's favorite flower because gladiolas are a popular flower in The Netherlands. I also love gladiolas because they have a regal aura about them. The large stalks of flowers, some intense bright colors, some soft subdued colors make for impressive bouquets that demand attention.

Gladiolas

38" x 56"

Fabric & Supplies

Refer to page 7 for recommendations on Fabrics, Tools, and Supplies.

Fabric Requirements

¾ yd – Background (black)
1¼ yds – Outer Border, and Binding (black)
½ yd – Inner Border (green)
¼ yd – Inner Border (red)
1/3 yd – Flowers (pink)
1/3 yd – Flowers (red)
¼ yd – Leaves (darker green)
¼ yd – Leaves (lighter green)
1¾ yds – Backing (color of your choice)

Hot Ribbon

2 pkgs – #1 White
3 pkgs – #2 Red
2 pkgs – #11 Lime Green
1 pkg – #13 Orange
2 pkgs – #14 Forest Green
2 pkgs – #17 Hot Pink

Copic Ciao Markers *(Optional)*

1 – YG63 Pea Green
1 – YG03 Yellow Green
1 – R29 Lipstick Red
1 – RV02 Sugar Almond Pink
1 – RV04 Shock Pink
1 – 0 Colorless Blender

Swarovski Crystals *(Optional)*

30 – #1 Dark Amethyst
20 – #13 Ernite
30 – #20 Light Amethyst
30 – #23 Lt Rose
50 – #25 Light Siam
75 – #18 Jet Black
30 – #14 Fire Opal (Large)
12 – #34 Dark Siam (Large)
25 – #42 Jonquil (Large)

Cutting Instructions

1. **Background:**
   Cut one 24" x 41" rectangle
2. **Red Inner Border:**
   Cut five 1¼" strips
3. **Green Inner Border:**
   Cut five 3½" strips
4. **Black Outer Border:**
   Cut six 4½" strips
5. **Binding:**
   Cut six 2½" strips

Constructing the Quilt

Refer to **The Hot Ribbon Applique Technique** on page 8 for step by step instructions.

Gladiolas Placement Guide

This diagram has been reduced.
Use for template placement only.

Enlarge Placement Guide 310%

15
16
B1
14
B2
19
Templates have been reversed for tracing purposes.
B7
B6
B5
13
B8
20
B4
21
29
B3

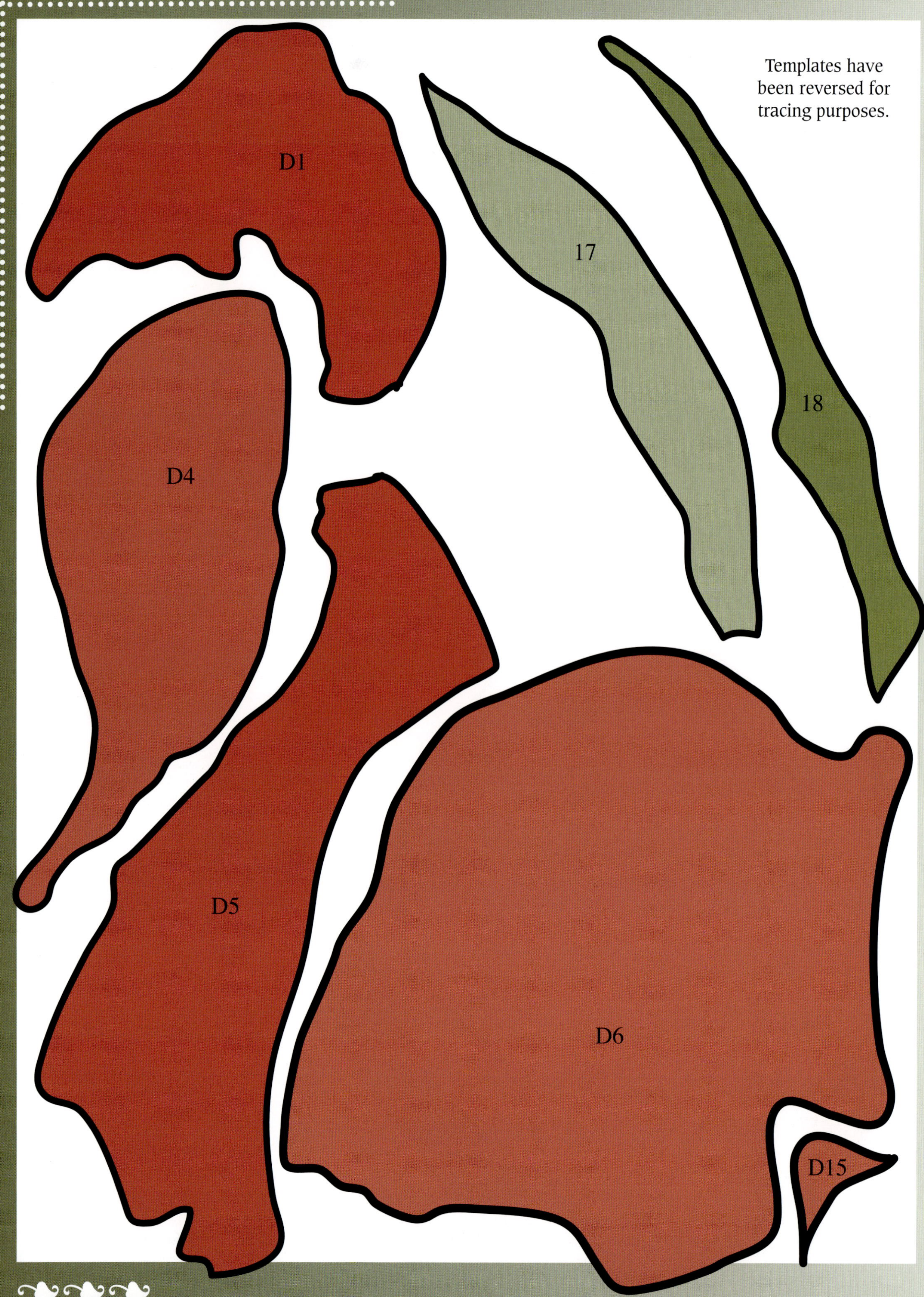
Templates have
been reversed for
tracing purposes.
D1
17
18
D4
D5
D6
D15

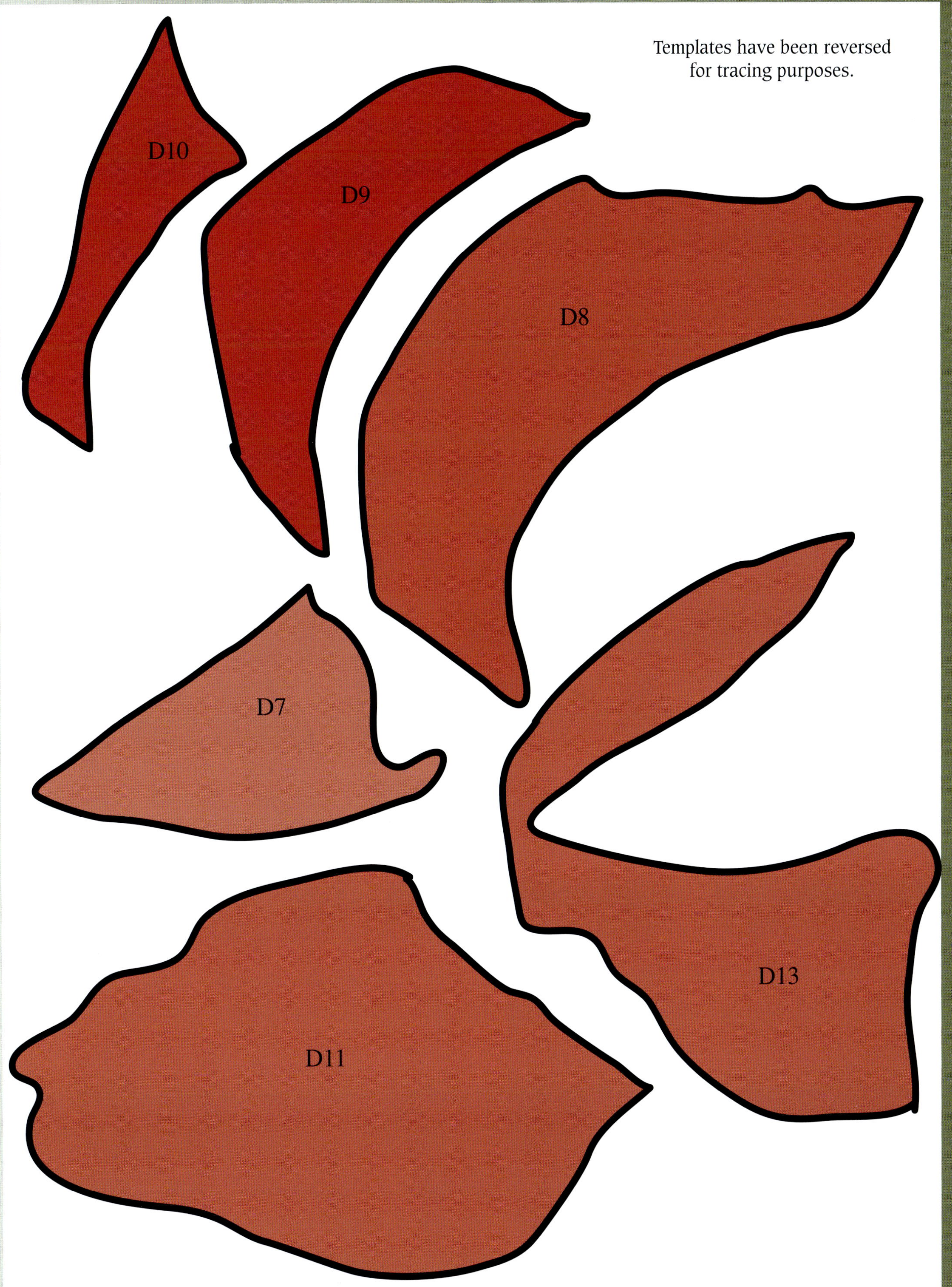
Templates have been reversed
for tracing purposes.
D10
D9
D8
D7
D13
D11

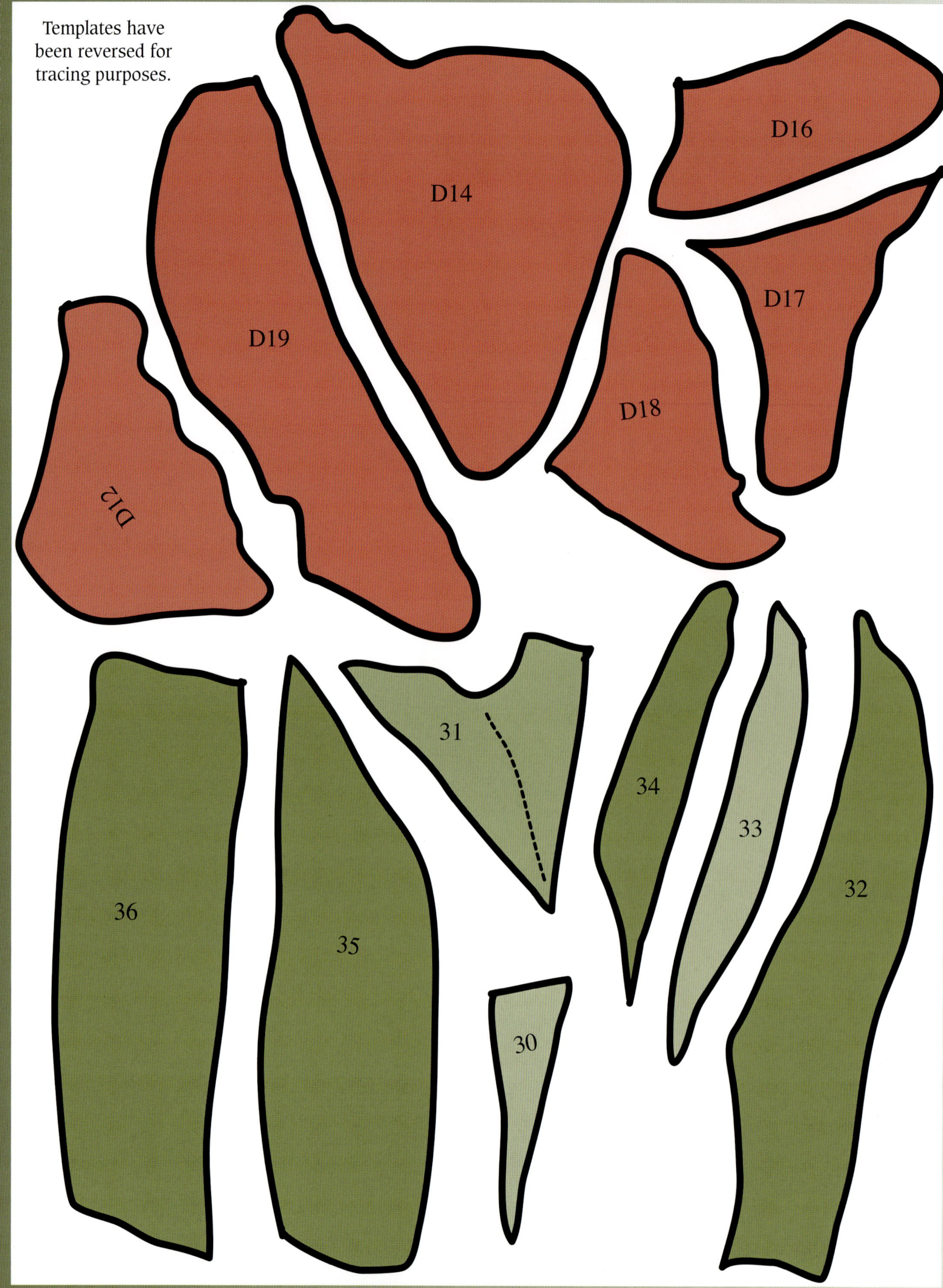
Templates have been reversed for tracing purposes.
D14
D16
D19
D17
D18
D12
31
34
33
32
36
35
30

Templates have been reversed for tracing purposes.

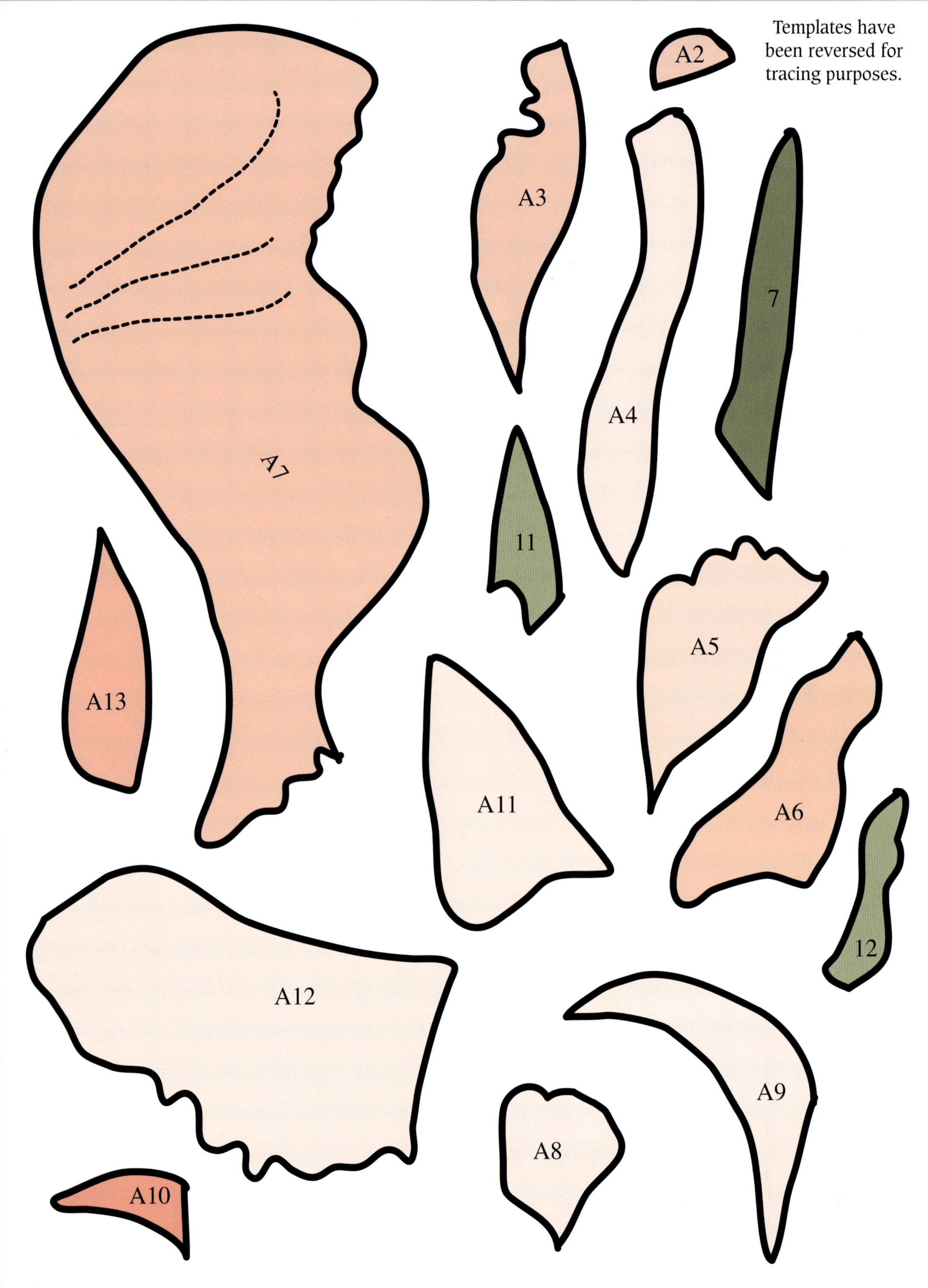
Templates have been reversed for tracing purposes.
A2
A3
A4
7
A7
11
A13
A5
A11
A6
12
A12
A9
A8
A10

Templates have been reversed
fortracing purposes.
A1
10
1
4
3
8
9
6
2
5

Hollyhocks

Hollyhocks are not very common any more which is probably why I had not seen one until about 2 years ago. I was driving along a narrow country road when I saw a large mass of pink flowers along the road next to a barbed wire fence in the middle of dry grass and dead weeds. The sight stopped me dead in my tracks! I was amazed not only by the beautiful flowers but more so by the contrast of a plant with lush green leaves and full of blossoms in midst of other plants that had died. I was impressed by the hollyhocks' resilience, toughness, and determination to survive in a harsh environment. That to me is what flowers can do - brighten up otherwise bleak places with a beauty beyond our expectations.

Hollyhocks

36' X 49"

Fabric & Supplies

Refer to page 7 for recommendations on Fabrics, Tools, and Supplies.

Fabric Requirements

1 yd – outer border and binding (magenta)

1¼ yds – background (mottled black)

¼ yd – inner border (light pink)

1/3 yd – inner border (green)

¼ yd – leaves (green)

½ yd – flowers (mottled soft pink)

1½ yds – backing (color of your choice)

Hot Ribbon

4 pkgs – #1 White

4 pkgs – #11 Lime Green

4 pkgs – #17 Hot Pink

Copic Ciao Markers *(Optional)*

1 – YG63 Pea Green

1 – RV02 Sugar Almond Pink

1 – RV06 Cerise

1 – BV00 Mauve Shadow

1 – 0 Colorless Blender

Swarovski Crystals *(Optional)*

100 – #19 Jonquil

50 – #28 Olivine

Cutting Instructions

1. **Background:**
   Cut one 26" x 39" rectangle

2. **Light Pink Inner Border:**
   Cut five 1" strips

3. **Green Inner Border:**
   Cut five 2" strips

4. **Magenta Outer Border:**
   Cut five 4" strips

5. **Binding:**
   Cut five 2½" strips

Constructing the Quilt

Refer to **The Hot Ribbon Applique Technique** on page 8 for step by step instructions.

Hollyhocks Placement Guide

This diagram has been reduced.
Use for template placement only.

Enlarge Placement Guide 250%

Templates have been reversed
for tracing purposes.

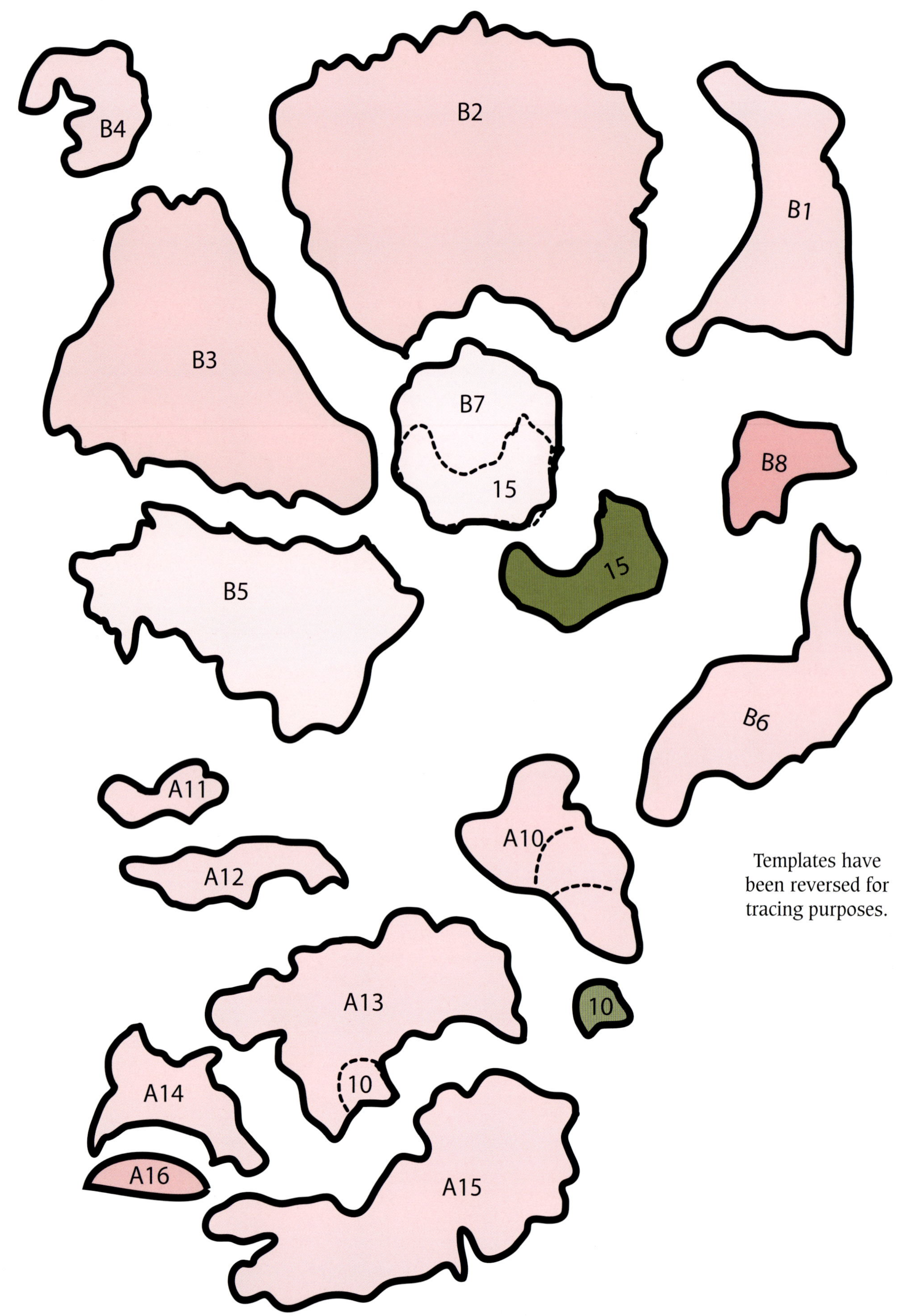

Templates have been reversed for tracing purposes.

Templates have been reversed for tracing purposes.
C1
C2
C3
C4
C5
C6
C7
C8
C9
C10
C11
9
11
12
17

16
14
13
Templates have been reversed for tracing purposes.
18
D2
D1
D4
D3
D7
D5
D8
D6
D9

Templates have been reversed for tracing purposes.

Gazinias

Gazinias are such a bright, cheerful flower that it's hard not to be attracted to them. Several years ago, our neighbor was not happy with the gazinias that he had in his yard and was planning to dig them out and throw them away. When we told him that we were looking for plants to fill a flower bed along our driveway, he gladly gave us as many plants as we wanted. The area is now a carpet of gazinias. They bloom constantly through the spring and summer and give us a lot of enjoyment. I was intrigued to find that gazinias close during the night and open again with the sun in the morning. Gazinias are a good reminder that there is a natural rhythm to life – there is a time to blossom as well as a time to rest.

Gazinias

40" x 40"

Fabric & Supplies

Refer to page 7 for recommendations on Fabrics, Tools, and Supplies.

Fabric Requirements

¾ yd – background (mottled burgundy)

¾ yd – outer border and binding (mottled burgundy)

¼ yd – inner border (green)

1/8 yd – inner border (yellow)

½ yd – flowers (yellow)

¼ yd – leaves (mottled green)

1¼ yds – backing (color of your choice)

Hot Ribbon

4 pkgs – #8 Lemon Yellow

3 pkgs – #14 Forest Green

Copic Ciao Markers *(Optional)*

1 – YG63 Pea Green

1 – YR16 Apricot

1 – Y38 Honey

1 – Y17 Golden Yellow

1 – 0 Colorless Blender

Swarovksi Crystals *(Optional)*

220 – #18 Jet Black

120 – #39 Topaz

Cutting Instructions

1. **Background:**
   Cut one 27" x 27" square
2. **Yellow Inner Border:**
   Cut four 1" strips
3. **Green Inner Border:**
   Cut four 2½" strips
4. **Burgundy Outer Border:**
   Cut four 4" strips
5. **Binding:**
   Cut four 2½" strips

Constructing the Quilt

Refer to **The Hot Ribbon Applique Technique** on page 8 for step by step instructions.

Gazinias Placement Guide

This diagram has been reduced.
Use for template placement only.

Enlarge Placement Guide 250%

Templates have been reversed for tracing purposes.

Templates have been reversed for tracing purposes.

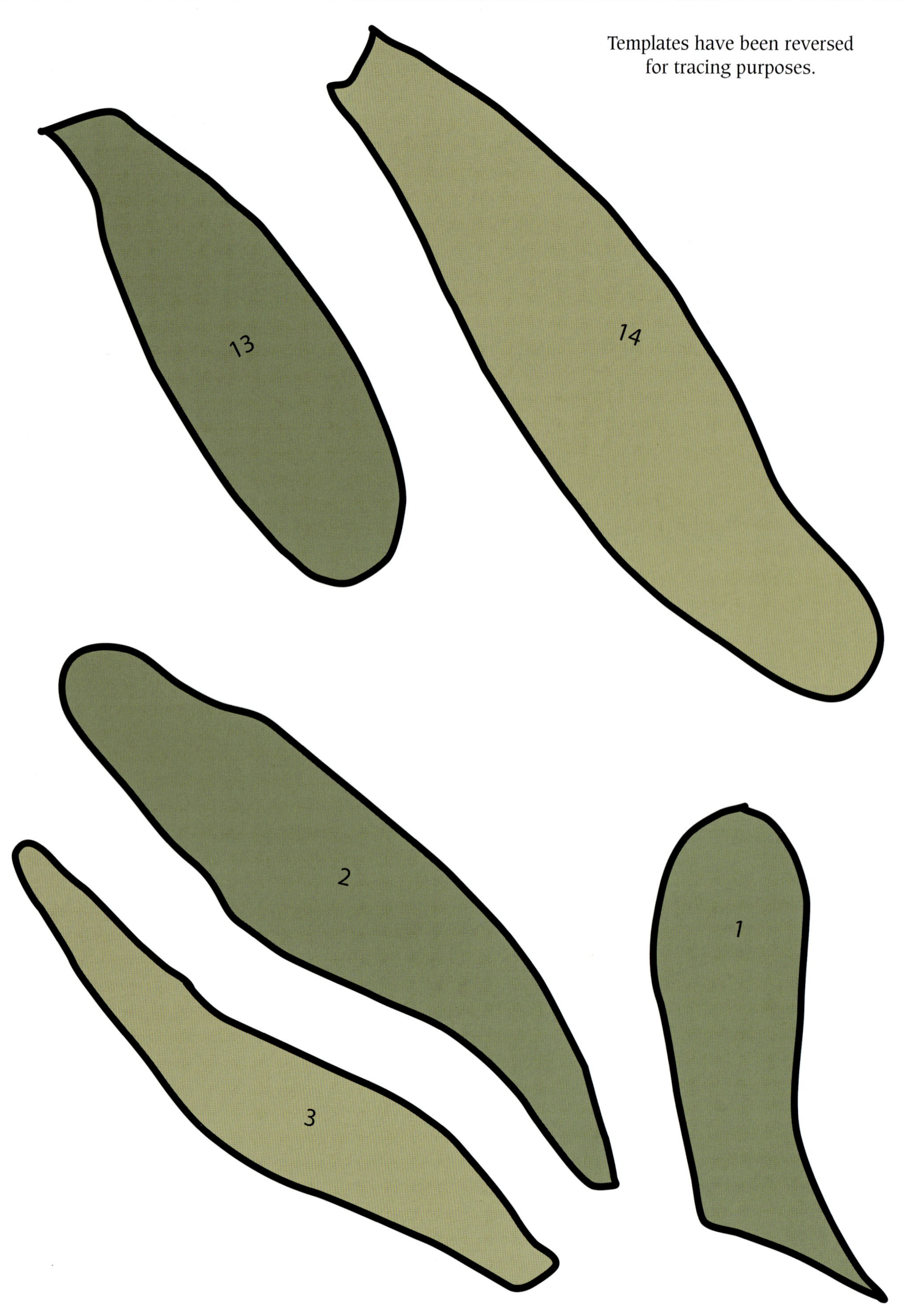

Templates have been reversed
for tracing purposes.

16

B2

17

B3

B1

B8

B4

B5

15

B6

B7

Templates have been reversed
for tracing purposes.
C4
C5
C6
C7
C8
C9
C10
9
10

Templates have been reversed for tracing purposes.

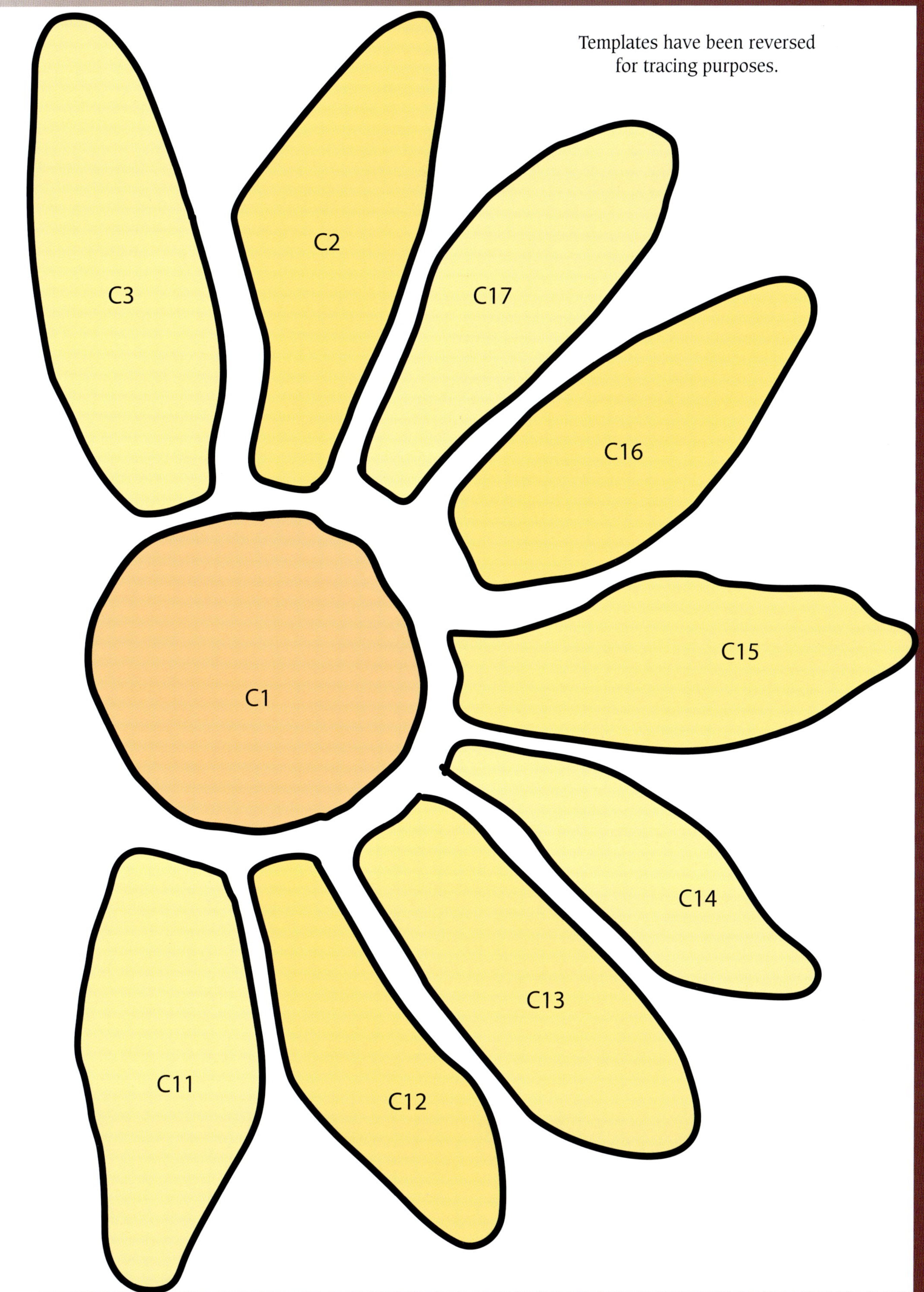

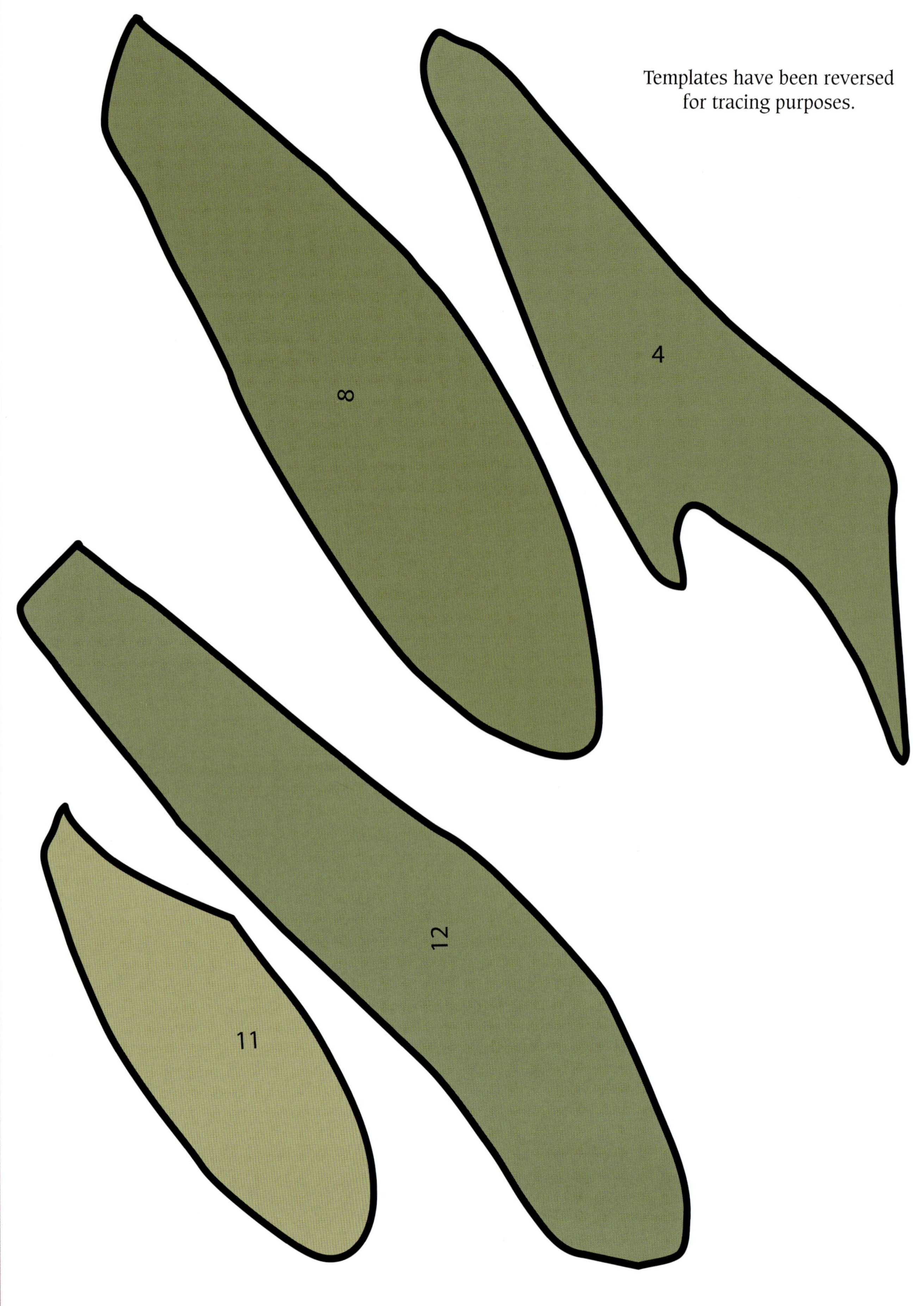
Templates have been reversed
for tracing purposes.
4
8
12
11

Templates have been reversed
for tracing purposes.
5
D4
D3
D5
D2
D15
D6
D1
D14
D7
D13
D8
6
7
D9
D10
D11
D12

Morning Glory

Morning Glory is regarded as a pest by many – you can't seem to kill it once it is established. But I like Morning Glory because I see it as a survivor. You can ignore it, you don't have fuss over it, and it rewards you with a profusion of flowers. We have several plants along our fence in the backyard and they have taken over our neighbor's tall bushes. Throughout the summer and fall, we have a wall of blue flowers that I can see from my studio window. Morning Glory may be a pest but pests can be beautiful if you take the time to look closely at it. It is a constant reminder to look for the beauty, the good in everyone, even those who we regard as "pests."

Morning Glory

36" x 38"

Fabric & Supplies

Refer to page 7 for recommendations on Fabrics, Tools, and Supplies.

Fabric Requirements

¾ yd – background (dark green batik)
¾ yd – outer border and binding (green)
¼ yd – inner border (fuchsia)
¼ yd – leaves (green)
3 fat quarters (pink, purple, & pale pink) – flowers
1¼ yds – backing (color of your choice)

Hot Ribbon

1 pkg – #1 White
2 pkgs – #7 Lilac
2 pkgs – #11 Lime Green
2 pkgs - #17 Hot Pink

Copic Ciao Markers *(Optional)*

1 – YG63 Pea Green
1 – RV04 Shock Pink
1 – V000 Pale Heath
1 – BV00 Mauve Shadow
1 – 0 Colorless Blender

Swarovksi Crystals (Optional)

100 – #18 Jet Black
85 – #13 Ernite
75 – #31 Rose
115 – #23 Lt Rose
60 – #11 Crystal
30 – #20 Lt Amethyst
25 – #1 Amethyst (Large)
25 – # 23 Lt Rose (Large)
25 – #42 Jonquil (Large)

Cutting Instructions

1. **Background:**
   Cut one 26" x 28" rectangle
2. **Fuchsia Inner Border:**
   Cut four 1½" strips
3. **Green Outer Border:**
   Cut four 4½" strips
4. **Binding:**
   Cut four 2½" strips

Constructing the Quilt

Refer to **The Hot Ribbon Applique Technique** on page 8 for step by step instructions.

Morning Glory Placement Guide

This diagram has been reduced.
Use for template placement only.

Enlarge Placement Guide 250%

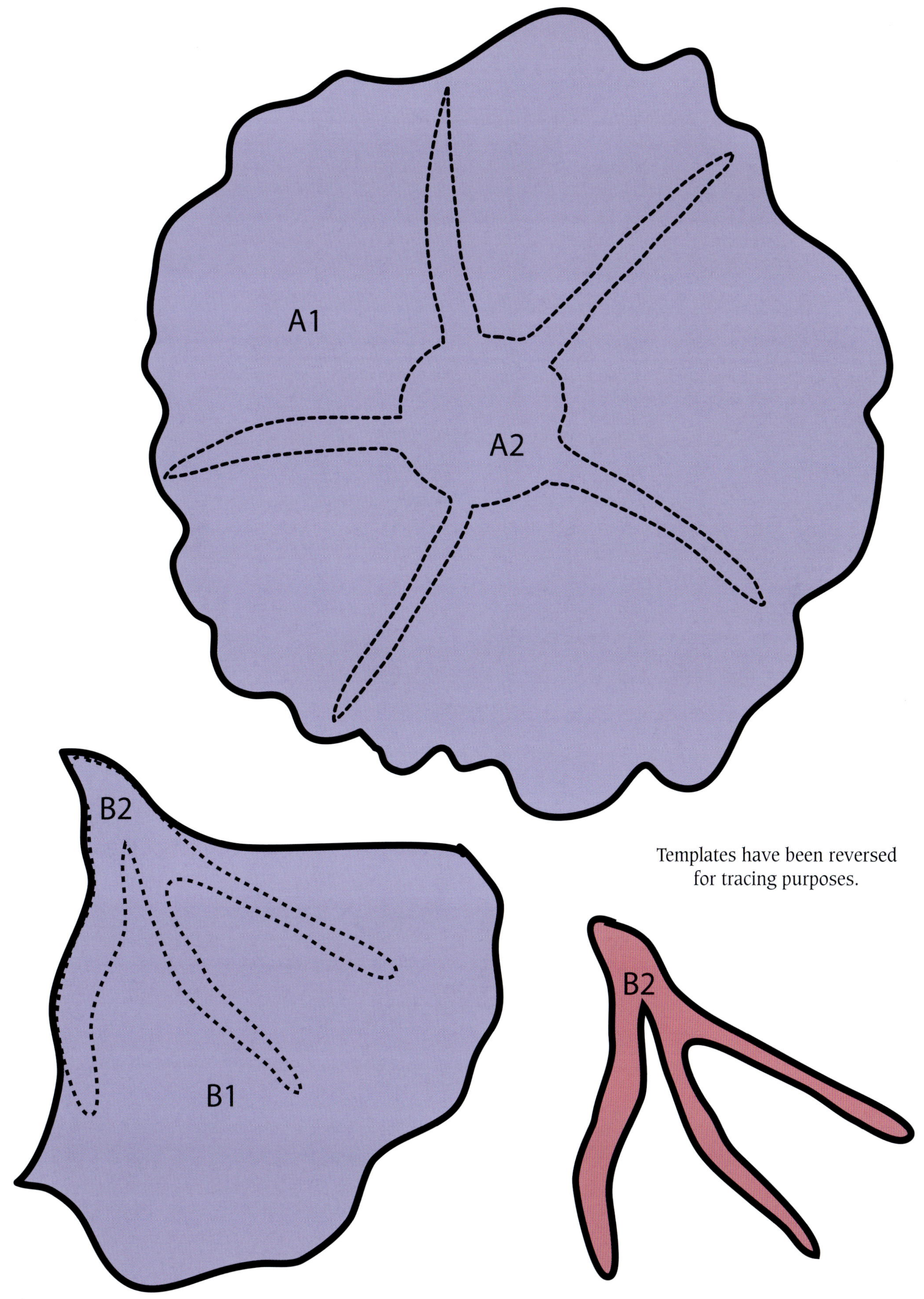

Templates have been reversed for tracing purposes.

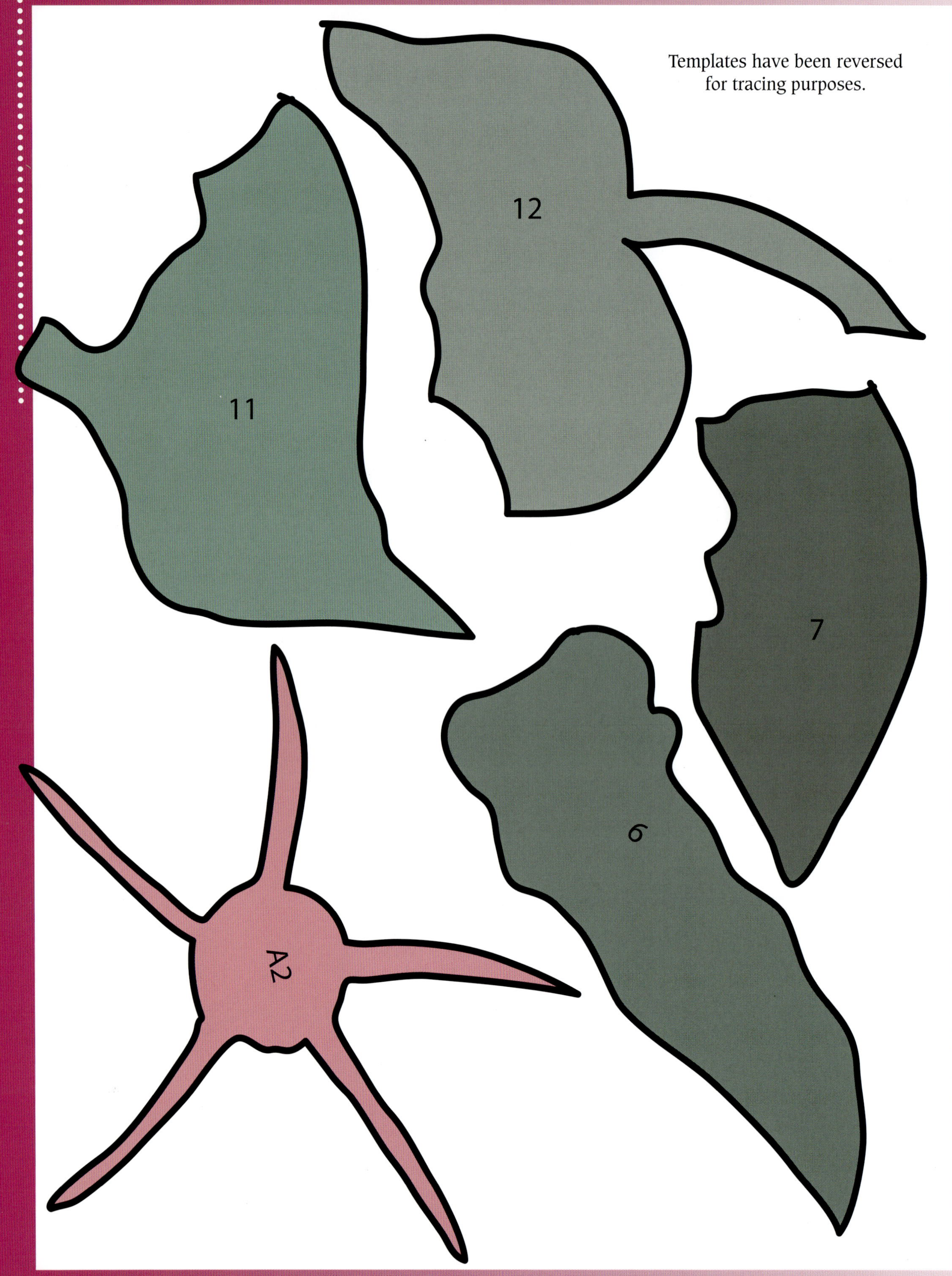
Templates have been reversed
for tracing purposes.
12
11
7
6
A2

Templates have been reversed for tracing purposes.

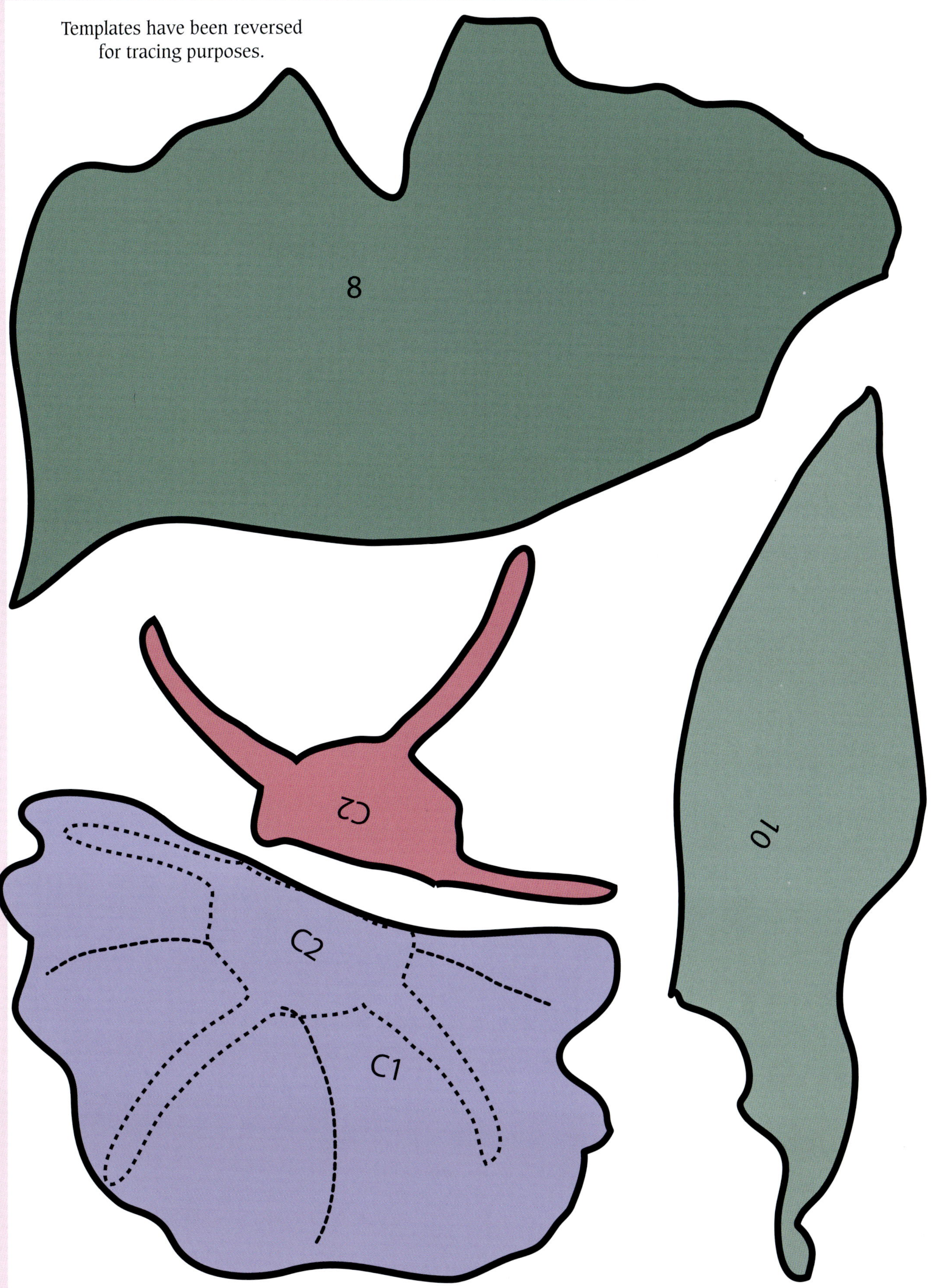

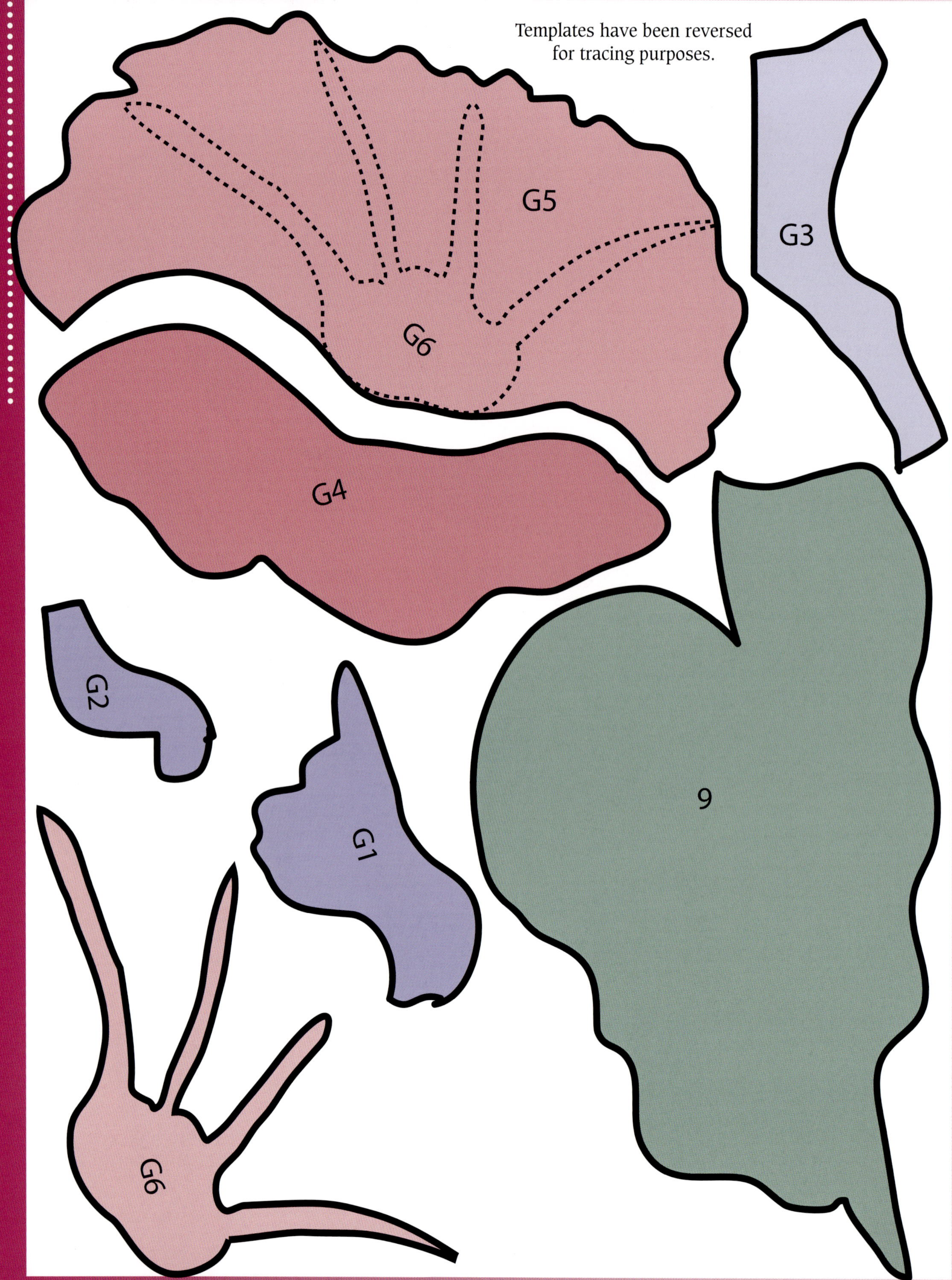
Templates have been reversed
for tracing purposes.
G5
G6
G3
G4
9
G2
G1
G6

Templates have been reversed for tracing purposes.

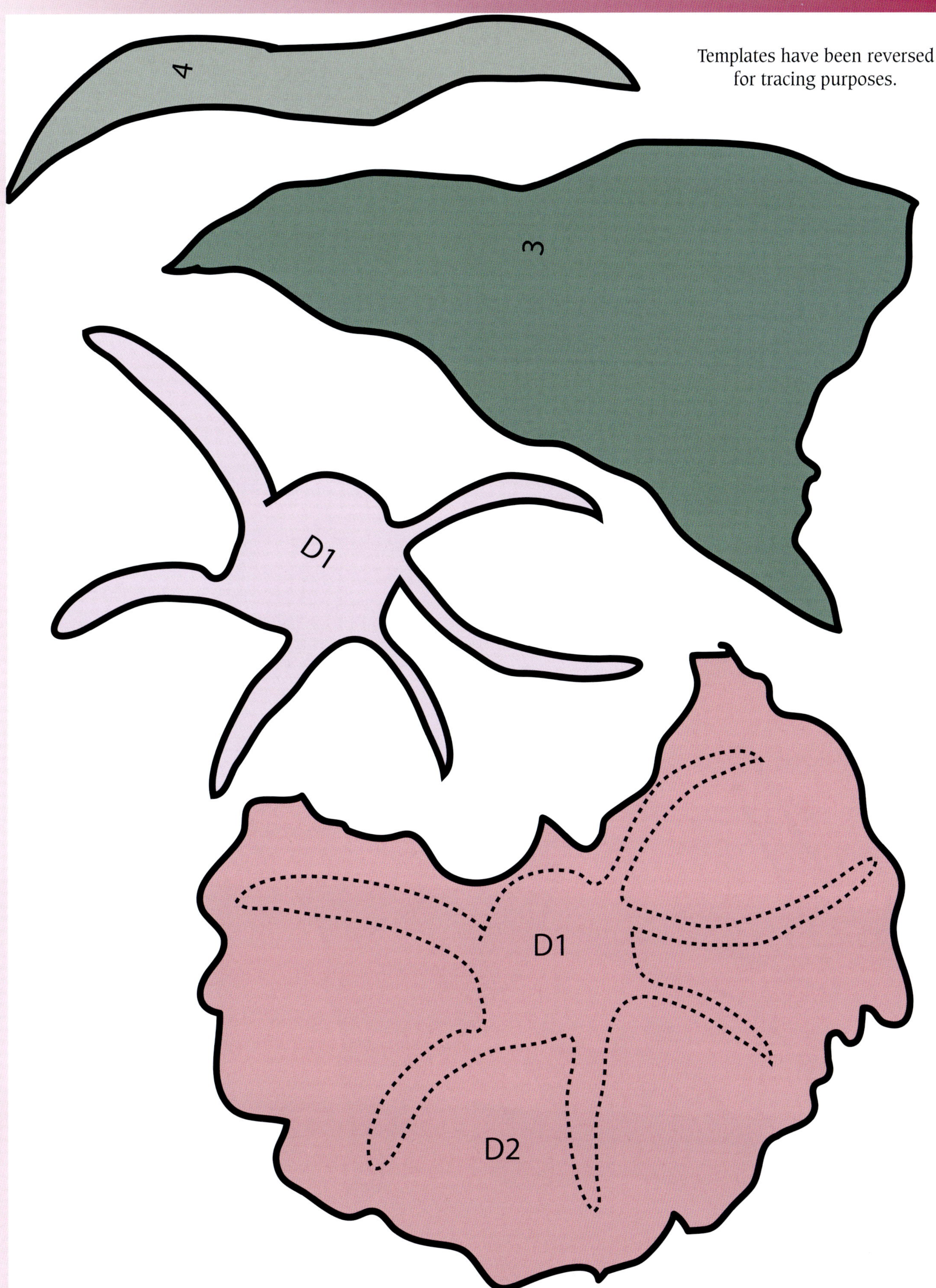

Templates have been reversed
for tracing purposes.

Templates have been reversed for tracing purposes.

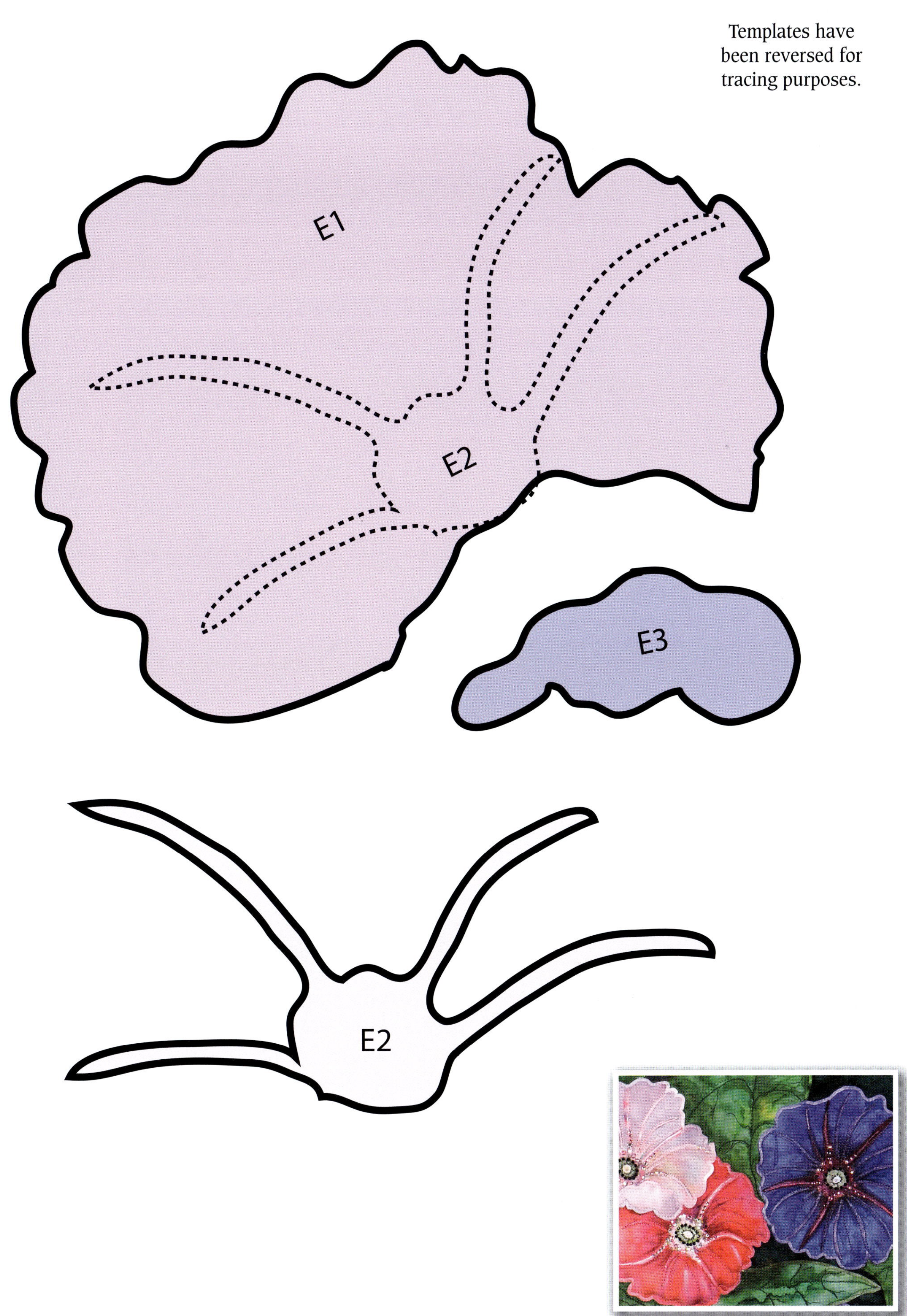

Nasturtiums

Nasturtiums reminds me of childhood vacations when we left the city (Rotterdam) and spent time on our family's boat that was in a marina on an island next to a farm. The farm had Nasturtiums growing around the barn and other buildings. I was attracted to the bright orange and yellow flowers and the unique leaves with the white stripes. They seemed to grow wherever there was even the smallest plot of ground. Although Nasturtiums were not highly regarded by many people then, I thought they were beautiful because of their simplicity and ability to grow anywhere. I forgot about Nasturtiums for many years until I saw them one day about 20 years ago. We were on vacation in British Columbia, Canada, where I was delighted to see masses of Nasturtiums in hanging baskets and spilling over retaining walls. I bought several packets of nasturtium seed and planted them in my yard. Although it is much hotter in California than The Netherlands, I'm pleased that I have been able to make them grow in my yard so I can enjoy them from early spring to late summer.

Nastartiums

27" x 27"

Fabric & Supplies

Refer to page 7 for recommendations on Fabrics, Tools, and Supplies.

Fabric Requirements

½ yd – background (dark mottled green)
¾ yd – outer border and binding (lighter gray-green)
¼ yd – inner border (orange)
Fat quarter – flowers (red)
Fat quarter – flowers (yellow)
Fat quarter – flowers (orange)
¼ yd – leaves (medium gray-green)
1 yd – backing (color of your choice)

Hot Ribbon

1 pkg – #2 Red
2 pkgs – #11 Lime Green
2 pkgs – #13 Orange
1 pkg - #19 Golden Yellow

Copic Ciao Markers *(Optional)*

1 – YG63 Pea Green
1 – YR16 Apricot
1 – Y17 Golden Yellow
1 – Y11 Pale Yellow
1 – R17 Lipstick Orange
1 – 0 Colorless Blender

Swarovksi Crystals (Optional)

10 – #11 Crystal
12 – #7 Citrine
12 – #48 Copper
18 – #18 Jet Black
4 – #42 Jonquil (large)

Cutting Instructions

1. **Background:**
   Cut one 18" x 28" rectangle

2. **Orange Inner Border:**
   Cut four 2" strips

3. **Gray-Green Outer Border:**
   Cut four 4" strips

4. **Binding:**
   Cut four 2½" strips

Constructing the Quilt

Refer to **The Hot Ribbon Applique Technique** on page 8 for step by step instructions.

TIP: I experimented with different ways to create the white veins in the leaves of the Nasturtiums. I found what works best is to dip a toothpick in bleach and, starting in the center of the leaf, carefully "draw" a line to depict the vein. Practice on a scrap piece of fabric until you discover the correct "speed" at which to apply the bleach so you get the result you want; if you go too fast, the line will not be visible; if you go too slow, the bleach will bleed too far and you will be left with a white blob and possible a hole in your fabric! IMPORTANT: When you have the result you like, blot the leaf with a damp towel to dilute/remove the bleach.

Nasturtiums Placement Guide

This diagram has been reduced. Use for template placement only.

Enlarge Placement Guide 200%

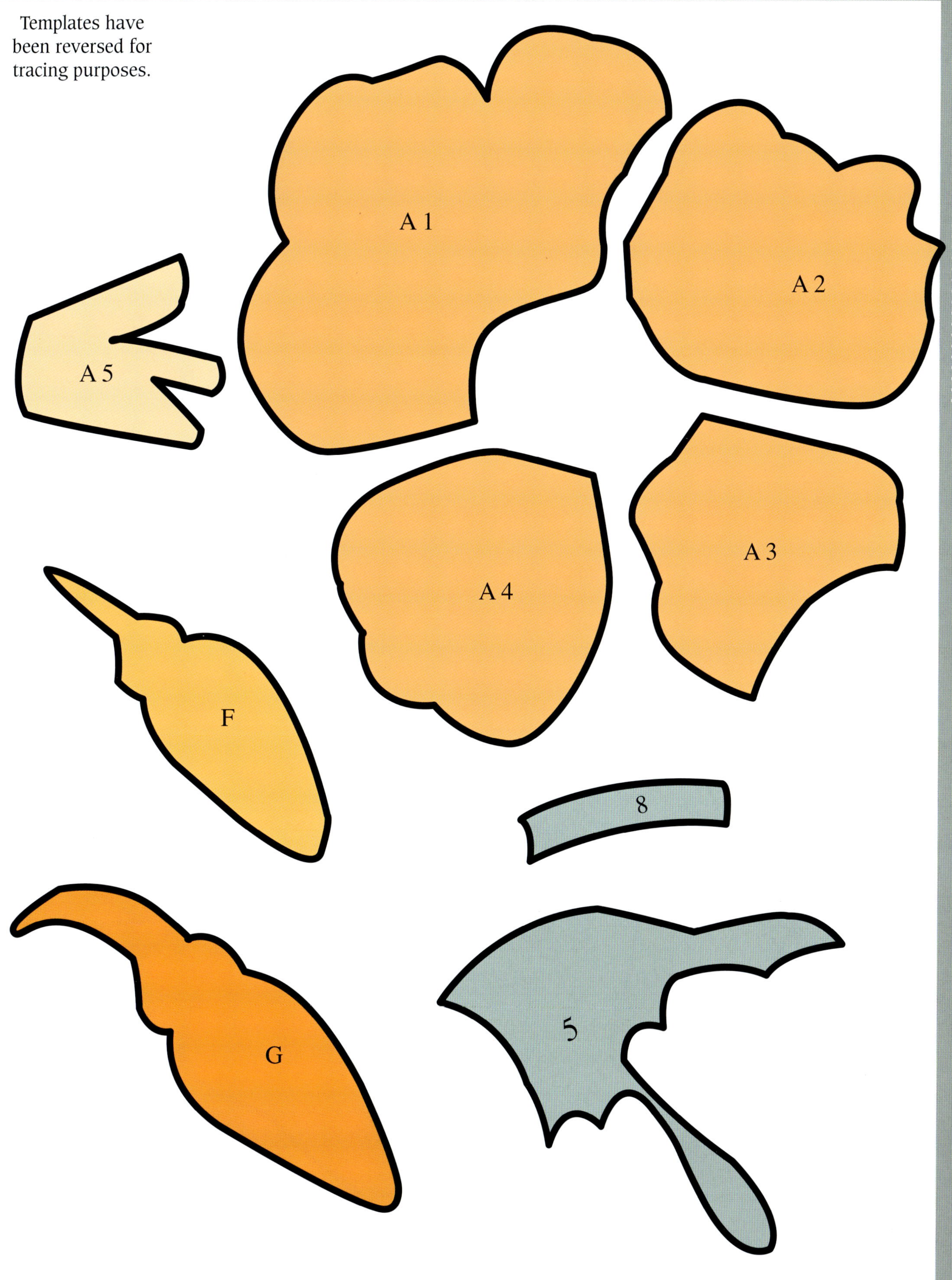
Templates have been reversed for tracing purposes.
A 1
A 2
A 5
A 4
A 3
F
8
G
5

Templates have
been reversed for
tracing purposes.
C1
C2
C2
E2
E1
H
D1
D2

Templates have been reversed for tracing purposes.

Templates have been reversed for tracing purposes.

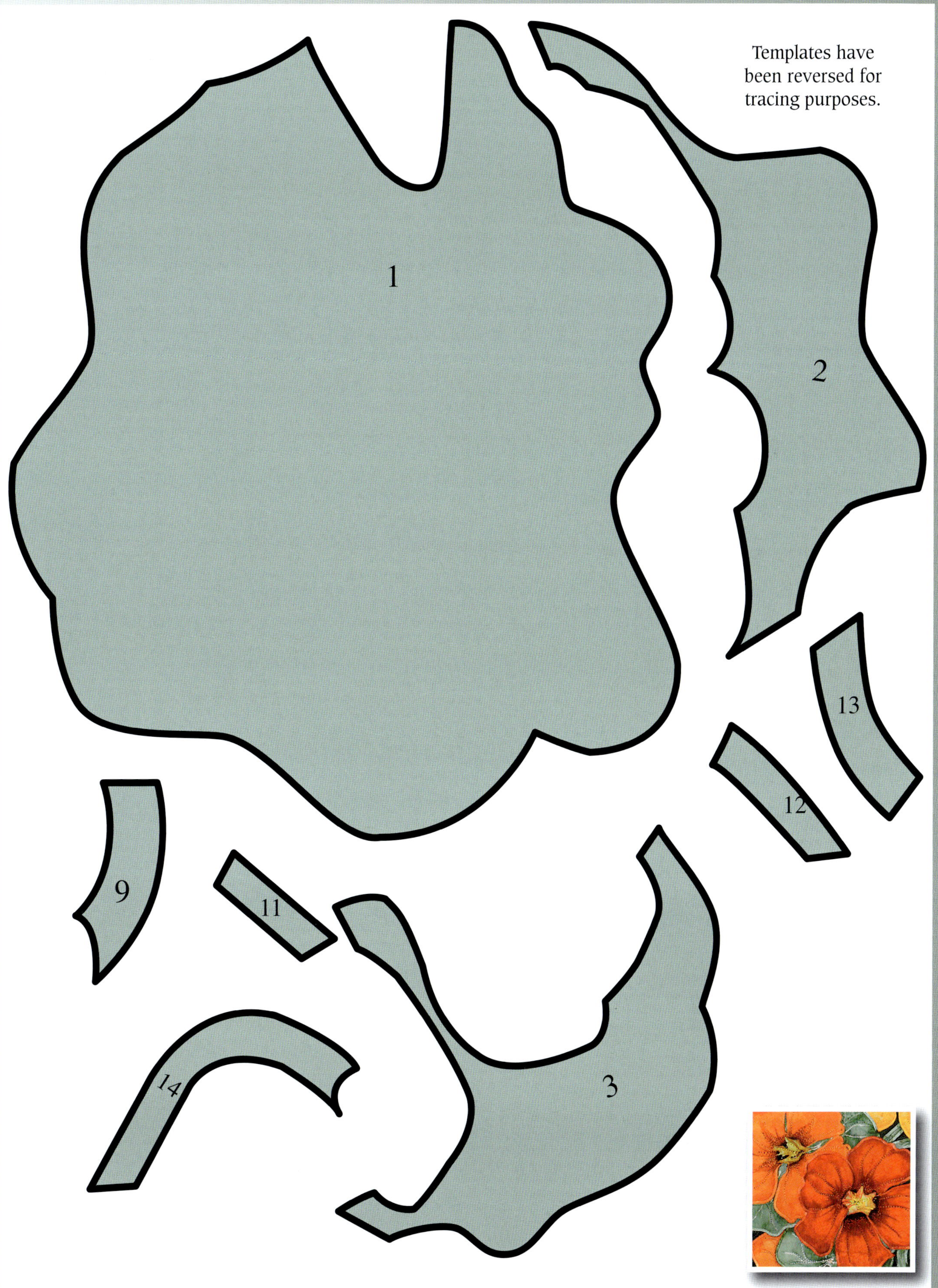
Templates have been reversed for tracing purposes.
1
2
13
12
9
11
3
14

Resources

(These companies generously provided their products for my use with quilting)

Imagination International, Inc. – www.hotribbon.com
Importer of Hot Ribbon and Copic Markers

Hoffman California Fabrics – www.hoffmanfabrics.com
Full-line fabric company

Baby Lock – www.babylock.com
Sewing, embroidery, quilting, and serger machines

Cheri's Crystals – www.cheriscrystals.com
Swarovski crystals

Dream World – www.dreamworld-inc.com
Bendable light, portable sewing machine tables

Bear Thread Designs – www.bearthreaddesigns.com
Appliqué pressing sheets

The Warm Company – www.warmcompany.com
Steam-a-Seam2

Ergonomic Advantage – www.ergonomicadvantage.com
Ergonomically correct sewing chairs

Mary Ellen Products – www.maryellenproducts.com
Spray starch alternative

Superior Threads – www.superiortheads.com
Extensive line of threads for top quilting, sewing, and embroidering

For more information on my books, patterns, and kits, you can contact me at:

Lennie Honcoop
4105 Saul Court
Elk Grove, CA 95758
phone # 916-683-1215
or
www.dutchquilter.com
lennie@dutchquilter.com

Other Patterns and Books

Floral Patterns

Elegant Iris

Dutch Tulips

Golden Sunflower

Pansy Bouquet

Regal Roses

Festive Poinsettias

Spring Daffodils

Water Lily

Amaryllis

Summertime Petunias

Books

Wine Series

Wine in a Glass

Wine in a Crock

Wine Country Retreat

Wine from Italy